American Oak Furniture

Styles and Prices

Robert W. and
Harriett Swedberg

Other books by Robert and Harriett Swedberg
  Off Your Rocker
  Victorian Furniture Styles and Prices, Book I Revised
  Country Pine Furniture Styles and Prices
  Victorian Furniture Styles and Prices, Book II

Library of Congress
Catalog Number 81-50507

ISBN 0-87069-363-8
10 9 8 7 6 5 4 3 2 1

Cover photograph: Bob Calmer
Cover design: Jann Williams Design
All other photographs by Authors
Printing and enlarging: Tom Luse

Published by

Wallace-Homestead Book Company
1912 Grand Avenue
Des Moines, Iowa 50305

To the two loved sons our daughters brought into our lives —

Terry Grant Watson and Michael Terry Jamison.

Acknowledgments

The authors are exceedingly grateful to those who generously shared their knowledge and gave of their time to help make this book possible. Most of the shops where photographs were taken offer a general line of merchandise. While they display oak, they do not specialize in just this one wood. Our thanks go to all who assisted, including those who did not wish to have their names listed.

Bob Anderson
The Antique Scene (Lamont and Lillian Hultgren), Moline, Illinois
Banowetz Antiques (Virl and Cathy Banowetz), Maquoketa, Iowa
Brightview Interiors, Antiques and Collectibles (Evelyn Maxwell), Milan, Illinois
Bill and Dot Best
Denise Brown
Mr. and Mrs. Ralph O. Clark
Ralph Crafton
Russ and Judy Day
Rev. and Mrs. Kenneth Douglas
Madge Foulk
Martha and Wilbur Gibson
Bob and Mary Grueskin (The Antique Scene), Moline, Illinois
Mr. and Mrs. Byron Hansen
Dee and Bernard Harding
Ron, Nancy, Shane, and Seth Harness
Hillside Antiques (Estelle Holloway), Frankfort, Illinois
Historic House Ltd. (Dale and Teresa Hoffman), Moline, Illinois
The House of Stuff 'N Things (Ann Figg), Buffalo, Iowa
Carole Hyler
Mike and Cheryl Jamison
Rosemary and Howard Johnson
LaMere's Furniture Stripping (Leslee and Duane LaMere), Rock Island, Illinois
Rose Lang
Gary and Lorraine Lynch
Mr. and Mrs. James L. Mc Daniel

Miller's Antiques and Collectibles, Bedford, Pennsylvania
Howard Moore
Parcel and Harker, East Moline, Illinois
Terry, Gretchen, and Andy Poffinbarger
Randy's Antiques (Randy Bahnsen, Owner)
Robbie's Antiques (Earle and Betty Robison), Lewisburg, Ohio
Anne Ross
Sewing Bird Antiques (Don and Helen Schwenneker), Cordova, Illinois
Charlie and Helen Shaffer
Rick Shunick
Mr. and Mrs. C. A. Siegfried, Jr.
Stanley's Antiques, Rock Island, Illinois
Towne Wood Shoppe (Keith and Shirley Miller), Deposit, New York
Traveler's Treasure (Fred and Diane Thomas), Deposit, New York
Pat and Mike Voss
Terry, Karen, Cody, and Adam Watson

Contents

Roman chair with medallions, head carvings, claw feet, 24½" wide, 15" to seat, 38" high, **$175-225.**

1 Pricing Oak Furniture

"I wish I could buy pottery at these rates!" a young collector remarked as she slammed closed a ceramic guidebook, her tone full of reproach because she felt the pottery pictured was marked too low.

Pricing is difficult, and facts about how it is done sound repetitious. But the conclusion is always the same. A price book is merely a guide.

Frequently one overhears that articles at a recent antique show were marked extremely high. Conversely, people will brag that items at an auction went very low, and that they were able to acquire treasures at bargain prices. Who is present and how desirable a specific article is help determine the cost. Perhaps if there had been someone seriously competing, the original bidder would have continued fighting upward, encouraged by the talented, cheerleader-type coaxing of the rapidly chanting auctioneer and the greedy desire he kindles in listeners to take home the prize. Because of this fostered rivalry, people are more apt to exclaim, "You can't buy anything at an auction. Bidders pay even more than they would in shops!"

Participants should decide ahead of time what a fair market value is or how much they can afford to spend, and not permit themselves to be chided into exceeding that amount. It is possible for neophytes to bid against themselves, so it is good to become familiar with the action before jumping in. Naturally, items should be inspected for flaws before the singsong pitch commences or the mallet bangs down. While auctions help to establish price trends, they are not a reliable measure of what an object sitting on a store shelf should cost.

There are legitimate questions a dealer may mull over as he puts a price tag on his merchandise. How much was paid for the piece? Would a replacement cost more? What is the current market value? Is the item in good condition? Does it require cleaning, repairing, or refinishing? Has it been altered in any manner — cut down, a new drawer added, the top replaced, a leg repaired? How rare is it? How old is it? Are there buyers who want it? Is it something with general appeal? Will it sell readily? Supply and demand is an ever-changing factor. An article may be both rare and old, but if no one wants to give it a home, its price will reflect this. There must be both a buyer and a seller.

Stand with slight warp and stain in top, painted, splayed turned legs, top 16″ square, 29½″ high, **$35-55.**

Stand with cabriole legs, molded apron, scalloped shelf, top 12″ square, 28″ high, **$95-115.**

Look at the two tables pictured. You can easily see that the stand on the right is in better condition than the one on the left, which has a warped, stained top and painted legs. Stylewise, the table on the right is more attractive because it features gracefully curved legs, while the table on the left has legs that are splayed and turned. Isn't it obvious that the table on the right has more value than the one on the left? One could be put to use immediately, while the other requires work before it can enhance a home's decor.

To an antiquer, a "marriage" refers to the uniting of two unrelated objects to make a whole. A buyer should be told of a marriage whenever the seller knows of one. Here is a well-designed buffet with scrolled feet and convex rolled drawers projecting over two doors. The quarter-sawed pattern is pleasing as it shows the

Buffet, quarter-sawed oak, replaced mirror back, 60″ wide, 20″ deep, 39″ high, base only, **$275-325.**

oak's medullary (pith) rays in a pronounced manner. However, the original top was missing and a mirror which has not yet been refinished was added to this piece to make a marriage. It is necessary to take such a change into consideration when pricing an object.

The next article has gone through a metamorphosis also. By cutting off the pillars, this substantial former library table has shrunk to coffee table height. How would you price such a transformation?

Library table cut to coffee table height, 42″ wide, 26″ deep, 18″ high, **$325-375.**

Ornate parlor armchair, oval back with floral crest, splayed legs, H stretchers, 27½" wide, 17½" to seat, 39" high, **$175-225.**

Because customers often feel free to ask for discounts, some shopkeepers add a substantial markup so that they can afford to haggle. People do not often request discounts in retail shops which normally mark their wares up 100 percent (buy for fifty dollars, resell for ninety-nine fifty). Besides, the merchants dealing in new commodities can reorder when necessary. They do not have to scrounge to find their products as an antiques dealer does, or clean them if necessary, or perhaps keep them on hand for years before they sell. In general, prices are escalating. Why should this increase not be acceptable in the antiques field?

Here is another approach. "This is my guesstimate," stated a former antiques dealer, now an oak addict, as he priced an unusual early 1900s parlor chair, a collectible. His coined word clings in his listener's memory as tenaciously as a carelessly discarded wad of chewing gum clings to the bottom of one's shoe. Pricing frequently does depend on educated guesses.

A price guide author writes down winning bids at auctions, notes prices at estate sales, in shops, malls, shows, and at flea markets, consults with owners and dealers, chats with collectors, reads ads in publications, speaks with travelers, and journeys to note prices in areas other than his own. Carefully prepared questionnaires may aid in research, and the state of the economy is an influencing factor. Even with this studied background, the appraisal of antiques and collectibles varies greatly. A prestigious, long-established, multibuilding shop may list items higher than a new, one-room store dares to demand even when the two operate in the same general locale. There are variations in values from shop to shop. There are regional differences also. Turn-of-the-century oak commands a high price in the Southwest and on the Pacific Coast. Usually, prices are deflated in the East. The Midwest has been the buying center for promoters from the West and South, but many shop owners in the Midwest now state that gas costs have severed their trade from these other sections. Semitrailer trucks are not rolling in from the Coast or the South to seek stacks of furniture as they once did. Soon this switch in purchasing practices may be reflected in the oak prices.

New round pedestal table, claw feet, **$300.**

New pressed back chair with spindles, plank seat, **$85 each.**

New pressed back chair with spindles, plank seat, set of 6, **$485.**

Getting something for free is fun and fair. For a start, the uninitiated seeker should search in Grandpa's shed or Grandma's attic for gift hand-me-downs. Sometimes a yard or estate sale may offer a bargain, as could a flea market display. For the novice, however, a reliable dealer is usually a safe choice. The newcomer wants time-past articles, not new, production-line furniture, and facsimilies *are* being manufactured currently. Some shops intermix the new with the old. Others plainly mark tags "new" when they sell such merchandise.

Remember, buyers should know that a price book is merely a guide. The furniture pictured therein is ordinarily available to the general public and not of museum quality. There are a few exceptions. With these reminders, may this price guide be your helpful handbook.

2 The Hardy Oak and Its Look-alikes

Oak—sturdy, staunch, heavy, hard, hearty—that's oak. Literature has contributed to the belief that oak is strong, since the mighty tree from a tiny acorn grows. Its kissing cousin, the chestnut, is depicted as a gracious, majestic giant by Henry Wadsworth Longfellow in his poem "The Village Blacksmith." "Under the spreading chestnut tree the village smithy stands...." The gentle guardian shades visitors while a burly blacksmith sweats over his flames and anvil, pounding out glowing iron to shape wagon parts, farm tools, kitchen utensils, fireplace accessories, or shoes for horses. Appropriately, it was actually a horse chestnut tree that inspired Longfellow.

Three-quarter bed, mixed woods. Many beds were made of ash with walnut trim, 52" wide, 81" long, **$350-400.**

In addition to chestnut, ash, elm, and hickory resemble oak yet have distinguishing characteristics of their own. Occasionally devotees might be surprised and perhaps not too pleased to realize that some of their "oak" really isn't oak at all. Pieces of furniture representing as many background blends as a mongrel mutt do exist. Oak does not bend well, thus parts such as the rounded back frames on chairs are frequently formed of the more relaxed elm or hickory. Since oak tends to splinter when held to a lathe, its use is avoided for turnings. Many "oak" iceboxes are actually ash or elm. If one does not desire to be precise, it is easier to permit these look-alikes to pass for oak, especially when dealers and collectors frequently err in their identity and label them incorrectly.

Windsor-type chair (commonly called captain or bar), usually of mixed woods since elm and hickory bend well. A soft wood could be shaped for the seat, and plain rungs were often made of oak, **$120-155.**

Chair with cane back and seat, made of mixed woods, 21" wide, 17" to seat, 36" high, **$200-250.**

Definition of Terms

A discussion of terms used in this book will promote a greater understanding of woods.

Annual rings are a tree's concentric yearly growth rings. They go round and round inside the tree trunk in a bull's-eye fashion.

Grain is the arrangement and direction of fibers in wood which give the wood its markings or texture. "Always sand with the grain of the wood, not across it, to prevent scratches" constitutes a woodworking rule.

Medullary or pith rays radiate from the center of the tree, almost in the way a kindergartner draws a yellow sun with straight yellow lines shining from it in octopus fashion. Oak's pith rays are referred to as flakes.

Pores are small openings for the absorption and discharge of fluids. When these can be seen readily, the wood is referred to as open-grained. Closed grain indicates difficult-to-spot pores.

Plain-sawed refers to boards sliced from the whole log lengthwise in parallel cuts. Stripes and a series of elliptical V's are the resulting patterns.

Quarter-sawed is a term that comes from the early practice of cutting a log into quarters by splitting it in half lengthwise. Each half was then cut in half again. The four equal triangles were sliced into parallel boards almost at right angles to the annual growth rings. This method wastes wood and calls for extra processing which increases the cost but produces lumber which shrinks and warps less than plain-sawed wood. Also, quarter sawing vividly exposes the flakes or pith rays to produce a pronounced pattern.

Parlor table, plain-sawed showing elliptical v's pattern, splayed turned legs, top 23" x 24", 29½" high, **$85-110.**

Chiffonier, quarter-sawed showing medullary or pith rays (note hat cabinet), serpentine drawer fronts, 34" wide, 18" deep, 48" high, **$365-415.**

Parlor table, cloverleaf top and shelf, cabriole legs, quarter-sawed oak, top 24″ square, 29″ high, **$95-125.**

Chiffonier of quarter-sawed oak, serpentine drawer fronts, 34″ wide, 19″ deep, 47½″ high, **$225-275.**

Octagonal school wall clock is Japanese, **$150-190.** Ingram kitchenette shelf clock, **$125-165.**

Now that the descriptive terms have been defined, here are some characteristics of these five indigenous furniture woods.

Ash has a prominent grain which resembles oak. It is heavy, dense, and light-colored. Because of its great strength, ash was formerly used for wheels on wagons that rolled pioneers across America's plains. Many "oak" iceboxes are actually ash. Upholstery frames utilize this species' great strength, too.

Chestnut is grayish brown in appearance and has a coarse open grain. It is softer, lacks the large rays, and is not as structurally tough as oak. A fungus disease attacked and destroyed most of this nation's chesnut trees, but companies turned the carnage into profit by dubbing the lumber "wormy chestnut" and making attractive panels from it.

Elm bends with ease and lends itself well to furniture parts which must be curved. It is porous with an oaklike texture. Because the wood has pleasing figures and its tendency to warp needs to be controlled, it is a natural to use for veneers. It does not split readily, so turned parts can be fashioned from it. Seats of chairs were frequently constructed from this wood.

Ash washstand commode with incised lines, pressed brass backplates for bail handles, 31″ wide, 15½″ deep, 29½″ high, **$155-195.**

The back of the ash washstand commode.

Eastlake ash dresser, two decks, swinging mirror, applied carvings, candlestands, 37″ wide, 17″ deep, 75½″ high, **$450-550.**

Ash primitive drop-front desk, 43″ wide, 15″ deep, 49″ high, **$375-475.**

Eastlake marble-top washstand commode with mixed woods, including chestnut, oak, ash, burl veneer, chip carving, incised lines, 28″ wide, 16″ deep, 39½″ high, **$425-500.**

Elm kitchen cupboard, 40″ wide, 16½″ deep, 67¼″ high, **$385-450.**

Kitchen chair (bent backs were often made of hickory or elm), 17″ to seat, 36″ tall, set of 4, **$75-90 each.**

Desk chair with cane seat and back, swivels, can be raised and lowered (bent parts were often made of hickory or elm), 20″ arm to arm, **$215-260.**

Hickory is hard and refuses to work easily, but shares the color and texture of oak. It's strong, elastic, and good for bent parts, especially those which require both thinness and strength such as bow backs on chairs. In former years it was used to make staunch wagon wheel spokes. Today tough tool handles are made of hickory.

Oak is light in color, but heavy, hard, durable, coarse, and open-grained. Its large pores (openings) are readily seen. Very distinct pith rays (called flakes) show up in the quarter-sawed lumber and are the largest rays in any tree native to the United States. Oak was the favorite furniture wood from the late 1800s through the early 1900s. When plain-sawed, elliptical v's often are seen in the resulting pattern.

Shivering oak trees refuse to grow in extremely cold climates. Nevertheless, approximately two hundred and seventy-five varieties are rooted in many countries. There are sixty types in the United States, with only about fourteen selected for the construction of commercial furnishings. While these trees grow throughout the entire country, most furniture stock comes from east of the Great Plains.

Oak dining room chair, splat back, set of 4, **$55-75 each.**

Oak pressed back, plank seated chair, turned spindles, set of 6, **$110-135 each.**

Dresser, artificial grain made to resemble quarter-sawed oak, 44" wide, 23" deep, 75½" high, **$140-170.**

And here's a surprise sixth entry—**Artificial grain.** Yes! Artificial grain! Inexpensive woods with little or no pattern might be stained to emulate oak. Small-town hotels which required a commode in every room could buy such furniture more economically than they could oak. Families who wanted to be up-to-date, but could not afford genuine oak, could choose an imitation.

The replica *Sears, Roebuck Catalogue* for 1897, the style pacesetter for the masses, boldly presented elm or ash in an "antique oak" finish. At times, the base wood was not even specified, as in the case of a porch settee constructed of "the best selected material," finished in "antique oak." Consumers could obtain lawn chairs similarly garbed.

How do you dress elm or ash or other hardwoods in antique oak guise? David W. Kendall, one of Grand Rapids, Michigan's, first furniture designers, discovered the answer in the late 1800s. He observed that workers chewed tobacco, gauchely spitting the messy juice on the oak floors of the factories. This expulsion darkened the boards. Kendall tried rubbing a tobacco liquid on furniture, but the resulting nicotine stain was not permanent. It was better to employ chemicals to obtain the desired appearance. Jealous competitors christened this finish "mud," but they hastened to achieve a similar color when antique oak became a marketable commodity.

The 1908 Sears Catalog offered a new cupboard design in "hardwood with solid oak front, high gloss golden finish." Most of the iceboxes illustrated were made of elm with a similar treatment. Hotel commode washstands made of northern hardwood wore golden oak makeup. Factories continued to doll up light birch with her plain figure to represent the better-endowed, dark mahogany, so fake grains remained chic.

By 1927, thirty years after the first Sears description of "antique oak" finish furniture, dining room sets "soundly constructed of hardwood, in imitation quarter-sawed oak" were "good looking and thoroughly reliable." Golden or fumed finishes were prominent.

In order to detect faked graining, look at the inside of a solid wood (not veneered) drawer front and note whether the pattern has similar characteristics on both sides. On a stand or table, check underneath the top for this same purpose.

In addition to faked or real mahogany, another wood often used was bird's-eye maple with its pattern of eyelike markings. Oak and her look-alikes were the elite, however, and are the true concern of this book.

Buffet base from which veneer and artificial graining have been stripped (note that one door retains its quarter-sawed oak appearance), 46" wide, 20½" deep, 36" high, **$125-155.**

3 The Glow of Golden Oak 1890 to 1920

Golden oak. What an elegant sound that has. This title must have been inspired by a supersalesman who wanted to create allure and an aura for a wood which he hoped to promote as walnut's stand-in. Why? For several reasons. By 1880, the supply of walnut was almost depleted. Something was needed to replace it. Also, popularity is peculiar and fickle. People seeking new styles adopted oak as the pet wood of those who sought to be modern. Rich ornamentation with applied carvings bowed adieu, as simpler, less cluttered furniture gracefully entered the marketplace. King Dark Walnut was dead. Long live Light Oak.

Round pedestal extension table, 54″ diameter, **$390-460.**

If you desire to add to your knowledge of oak, visit Grand Rapids, Michigan, last century's furniture capital of the United States. Tiptoe into the research section of the downtown public library and whisper-talk with the knowledgeable staff. Their on file, original old catalogs are a trifle crisp and fragile but, when handled gently, will reveal a glimpse of yesteryear. Walnut eagerly dominates, but oak, a late 1800s newcomer, peeks into the records demurely.

Women's skirts were floor-sweeping long, and blouses were chokingly high at the throat back in 1890 when the Manestee Manufacturing Company in that Michigan city advertised an oversized golden oak sideboard with a top four feet long and almost three feet deep at the majestic price of fourteen dollars. It was finished in layers of shellac with a coloring agent added. After each layer dried, other layers were added, then rubbed to emit this golden glow. In 1893, the Widdicomb Furniture Company in Grand Rapids offered bedroom (bedchamber) and dining room suits (suites) in oak, bird's-eye maple, and curly birch. By 1895, Widdicomb's descriptive terminology switched to white oak, golden oak or birch, and mahogany, as people of the Gay Nineties updated their home furnishings, tossed out the clutter of the immediate past, and lightened their dark, heavily draped rooms to let the golden sunshine in.

Parlor table, brass claws, balls are missing, splayed legs with rope turnings, top 23½" square, 29" high, **$125-150.**

Pressed back chair, plank seat, turnings resemble stacks of coins, set of 6, **$145-170 each.**

Pressed back chair with pressed cane seat, set of 6, **$145-170 each.**

Generally, dining chairs (sometimes called diners) were not hand-carved, but had a design forced into the wooden slats with a metal die. These chairs are called "pressed backs." They can have solid plank seats, or they can feature cane, either hand-woven through holes in the seat frame, or made of a pre-woven material if a groove is present. Back in that time period, career women were not numerous, because, as any 1890s male could state, a woman's place was in the home. Using horse and wagon delivery and pickup, factories farmed out chairs which housewives caned for a small remuneration. Since child labor laws were almost nonexistent, little ones could, and did, assist.

Close-up of fish design pressed in the chair backs. Elaborate patterns such as this one are unusual and more costly.

Pressed back side chair, cane seat, fish design, set of 6, **$255-280 each.**

Pressed back armchair, cane seat, fish design, **$255-280 each.**

When the factory used pre-woven sheets, a piece was cut several inches longer on all sides than the seat hole. This was soaked in water until it became pliable. The caning was then stretched tautly over the seat opening, and the edges were pushed into the surrounding glue-filled groove in the frame. A spleen driven in on top held the cane taut. Any superfluous bits were trimmed off. This formed what is referred to as a pressed cane seat.

Round dining room tables with thick pedestal bases or rectangular tables with bulbous legs frequently divided in the middle and could be pushed outward for insertion of extra leaves to accommodate all the family home for a holiday. (Families tended to have more children then.)

In agricultural areas, neighboring farmers joined together as a traveling labor unit to help each other thresh their grain. The huge black vibrating threshing machine belched and spewed forth chaff. It had as insatiable an appetite as the workers who stopped at noon to devour the country buttered corn on the cob, crisp chicken, potatoes and gravy, succotash, thick tomato slices, green beans, homemade bread with fresh jelly, and plump fruit pies. The hostess had daughters who assisted, plus the farmers' wives, since threshing, despite the hard, hot work, was a social event. The noon meal at the golden oak extension table was a time for the men to chatter and tease as the women dutifully served them.

Round pedestal extension table, claw feet, 45" diameter, 28½" high, **$750-850.**

Boys helped, too, fetching water and caring for the teams of horses which pulled the wagons heaped with grain from the fields. It's remembering the past — history and heritage interwoven as tightly as the cane on the seats of the pressed back chairs—that makes collecting such endearing pleasure.

On farms and in cities alike, the dining room suite generally included a buffet (sideboard). Frequently these were very large. Features acclaimed were a lined, divided drawer for silver flatware and other drawers designed for linens. China and glass table services were confined to the cupboard section. China buffets with convex glass inserts displayed colorful plates or sparkling cut glass. Since these china buffets are now rare, they are coveted by serious collectors.

Buffet, convex projection drawers, scroll feet, 54″ wide, 23″ deep, 53½″ high, **$325-375.**

China cabinets almost burst with displays of hand-painted dishes. Many cabinets featured glass doors which literally bulged to present pregnant fronts.

But, as collectors today fully realize, not only were these china cabinets decorative, they were eminently practical. Treasured, fragile family possessions, safely on view to one and all, sparkled brilliantly in their strong, dustfree embrace.

China cabinet, convex (swell) glass on door and sides, 40″ wide, 14″ deep, 63″ high, **$525-600.**

Round pedestal extension table, claw feet, 45″ diameter, 28½″ high, **$625-725.**

Square extension table with five reeded legs, top 41½″ x 42″, 30″ high, **$250-300.**

Double pedestal extension table, square with rounded corners, veneered apron and pedestals, top 42″ x 42½″, **$650-700.**

31

Round pedestal extension table, 54″ diameter, 29½″ high, **$750-850.**

The same table shown with pedestal divided.

Square extension table, five turned legs, top 42″ x 42½″, 31″ high, **$245-295.**

Rectangular extension table, five legs, rounded corners, ball feet, 45″ wide, 49″ deep, 29¾″ high, **$285-345.**

Pedestal base for extension table, lion heads, claw feet. Shop price for complete table, **$1,950.**

Square extension table, five bulbous legs with reeding, top 45½″ x 45″, 30½″ high, **$450-550.**

Round pedestal table, plain lines, 42½″ diameter, 29½″ high, **$600-700.**

Square extension table with six bulbous reeded legs, concave stretchers with ball decorations, top 44″ x 43″, 29″ high, **$625-725.**

Round pedestal table, carving on edge of apron, claw feet, 45″ diameter, 30″ high, **$875-975.**

Round extension table, two auxiliary supporting legs drop down on each side when table is opened, scroll feet, 48″ diameter, 29″ high, **$475-575.**

Round pedestal extension table, claw feet, pedestal separates for support when additional leaves are added, 45″ diameter, 28″ high, **$675-775**.

Oval drop-leaf table, top 41″ x 22″, 31″ high, drop leaves 13″, **$275-325**.

Queen Anne leg extension table, two center legs remain stationary when leaves are added, label reads "Spencer Table and Chair Co., Marion, Ind.," top 45″ x 54½″, 29½″ high, **$425-500**.

Ornate pressed back chair, cane seat, set of 6, **$145-170 each.**

Pressed back chair, pressed cane seat, set of 6, **$125-145 each.**

Pressed back chair, cane seat, set of 4, **$145-165 each.**

Pressed back chair, set of 4, **$95-115 each.**

Pressed back chair, Man of the North Wind design, plank seat, set of 6, **$200-250 each.**

Close-up of Man of the North Wind.

Close-up of serpent-like medallion on chair back.

Pressed back chair, cane seat, set of 4, **$135-165 each.**

Pressed back chair, set of 6, **$60-75 each.**

Pressed back chair, cane seat, set of 4, **$145-170 each.**

Ornate pressed back chair, plank seat, set of 6, **$245-275 each.**

Close-up of winged creature and prey on pressed chair back.

Pressed back chair, cane seat, set of 4, **$135-160 each.**

Pressed back chair, set of 6, **$125-150 each.**

Pressed back chair, cane seat, set of 4, **$145-165 each.**

Pressed back chair, plank seat, set of 4, **$90-115 each.**

Pressed back chair, cane seat, set of 6, **$115-140 each.**

Pressed back chair, cane seat, set of 4, **$115-140 each.**

Pressed back chair, cane seat, set of 4, **$115-140 each.**

Pressed back chair, plank seat, set of 4, **$115-135 each.**

Ornate pressed back parlor chair, plank seat with corner scrolls, **$155-180.**

Spindle-back chair, cane seat, set of 4, **$115-135 each.**

Chair with arrowlike spindles, cane seat, set of 4, **$145-170 each.**

Spindle-back chair, cane seat, set of 6, **$115-140 each.**

Chair, plank seat, set of 6, **$95-120 each.**

Plain-back chair, plank seat, **$40-60.**

Veneered-back chair, round seat, **$35-50.**

Side chair with hand grip, round seat, **$75-95.**

Splat-back chair, cane seat missing, set of 6, **$75-95 each.**

Splat-back chair, seat missing, set of 6, **$55-70 each.**

Splat-back chair, leather seat, set of 4, **$65-80** each.

Splat-back chair, leather seat, set of 6, **$55-65** each.

Splat-back chair, upholstered seat, set of 6, **$55-65 each.**

Splat-back chair, leather seat, cabriole legs, set of 4, **$45-60 each.**

Buffet, cabriole legs, 37½″ wide, 18″ deep, 38½″ high, 7¼″ gallery, **$325-375.**

Buffet, gargoyle decorations on top rail, applied carved decorations, 48″ wide, 22″ deep, 80″ high, **$825-925.**

Ornate buffet, gargoyle decorations, applied carving, swell drawer fronts, 60″ wide, 25″ deep, 83″ high. Shop price, **$3,250.**

Buffet, base only, veneer removed from drawers, serpentine front, applied carvings, 48" wide, 23" deep, 30" high, **$250-300.**

Buffet, serpentine projection drawers, applied carvings, 42" wide, 20" deep, 62½" high, **$575-675.**

Buffet, projection drawers, applied carvings, 44" wide, 22" deep, 77" high, **$575-625.**

Unusual buffet, convex (or swell) front, beading trim, three-dimensional molding on doors, graceful and elegant, 58″ wide, 26″ deep, 65″ high, **$1,250-1,500.**

Buffet, applied decorations on doors, 46″ wide, 22½″ deep, 65″ high, **$375-475.**

China cabinet (or closet), fretwork at top of flat glass doors, scroll legs, 40″ wide, 13″ deep, 57¼″ high, **$375-450.**

China closet, leaded glass at top of straight glass doors, 40″ wide, 13″ deep, 59¼″ high, **$425-525.**

China closet, straight-lined, 40″ wide, 12″ deep, 62½″ high, **$325-400.**

China closet, beading across top, 39″ wide, 13″ deep, 48¾″ high, **$350-425.**

China closet, convex (swell) glass sides, straight glass door with muntins, 51½″ wide, 14″ deep, 55″ high, **$675-775.**

A golden glow radiated from the kitchen, also. When Hoosier cabinets were not factory painted, they appeared in this finish. Cupboards with glass doors in the top, drawers, and paneled wooden doors in the base received a golden finish, too.

Kitchen cupboard, incised lines, cornice, 40" wide, 19" deep, 83½" high, **$375-475.**

Kitchen cupboard, incised lines, cornice, 40" wide, 18½" deep, 83½" high, **$425-525.**

Corner cupboards are often as reluctant to stand in a corner as a recalcitrant child. No way can they be forced to share a space where heating, air conditioning units, windows, telephones, or other modern conveniences assume priority status.

Kitchen cupboard, cornice, three arches above top glass panes, 37″ wide, 16″ deep, 73″ high, **$275-350.**

Kitchen cupboard, screening added behind glass for privacy, replaced pulls, 37″ wide, 16″ deep, 69¼″ high, **$275-350.**

Ceiling height must be considered, too. Corner cupboards demand special spaces of their very own, and if you can't oblige them, don't bother to bring them home. These two cupboards found their niches. Both were treated to a golden oak finish.

Corner cupboard, wooden panels in top have been replaced with glass, 36″ wide, 20″ deep, 88½″ high, **$650-750.**

Corner cupboard, chamfer stiles, cornice, 45″ wide, 19½″ deep, 96½″ high. This cupboard would be too tall to fit in many modern homes, **$675-775.**

Farm lads helped their fathers and neighbors cut thick cubes of ice from frozen rivers when winter's continuous cold temperatures gave the waters a solid surface. These stored-up blocks would be available during the summer's heat. City kids had a different view of where ice came from. They raced after the wagon driven slowly down the streets by a hefty man who watched for an order card placed in a house window. When he saw a card, he would stop, get out, and plunge his ice tongs into the crystal dripping surface of a twenty-five, fifty, or seventy-five pound block, sling it over his shoulder, and carry it inside for insertion into the icebox. While he was gone, the youngsters sought momentary coolness by clambering on the wagon to find small pieces of crystal ice to suck. Would you believe the icebox shown here is actually still in use? The owners stated that it is difficult to secure block ice which will keep in the insulated compartment for several days. Cubes melt faster. If the

Icebox, actually in use as a refrigerator at present, label reads "Lapland Monitor, The Ramey Refrigerator Co., Greenville, Mich.," 35" wide, 19½" deep, 48" high, **$525-625.**

drip pan that catches the runoff is neglected and not emptied, a mop-up job is required. The only energy necessary to run this refrigerator is manpower to haul, fill, and empty the overflow container. Most iceboxes serve only as novelty storage units today. Many are constructed from elm or ash and dressed with a golden oak look.

Petite icebox, label reads "American House Furnishing Co.," 20½" wide, 14" deep, 37" high, **$400-475.**

Icebox, zinc interior intact, handle automatically closes, 26" wide, 18½" deep, 47½" high, **$375-450.**

Icebox, lift-lid for ice compartment, molded panels, label reads "Cold Storage," 28" wide, 17" deep, 43" high, **$475-550.**

The parlor provided a special place to entertain guests, and "matching" was the word as the 1800s closed. All the component parts of a parlor set were similarly styled. There was a sofa, platform "easy" rocker, an arm and two side chairs in a five-piece set. If you went for six pieces, a divan (love seat size) was added. Despite exposed wood and plump padding, a fragile appearance prevailed in the sofa and divan. Other rockers and fancy chairs invited people to sit. By the 1920s, davenports with a massive stuffed appearance along with various stocky chairs and rockers composed a hefty set which sometimes projected a Mission feel. The golden oak finish still appeared, but was fading out as veneered walnut and mahogany and the overstuffed, fat furniture waddled in.

Platform rocker, applied beading and carving. (Parlor suites frequently included a platform rocker, two side chairs, an armchair, and a sofa.) 23" arm to arm, 38" high, **$215-265.**

Tables with specific duties abounded. A fern with delicate tracery might droop around a taboret (or tabourette, if you want a fancy spelling for this flower stand). Lamps (frequently kerosene rather than electric, especially in rustic locales) perched on small parlor tables. A library-type table held accumulated literature, and bookcases stood nearby. Tall secretaries, a combination bookcase-desk, were common additions. Later, many bookcases came in sections and could be placed one on top of another in much the same way a child builds with blocks. The base frame and top cornice were separate units. Glass doors lifted up and slid inside to disappear when opened. Dainty desks, specially for the ladies, frequently featured cabriole legs, the chic French bowed look. Roll-types, at times referred to as "curtain tops," generated a manly appearance.

Bookcase with doors that pull up and slide in, used as a china cabinet. Each shelf is a separate unit stacked on top of another, 11" high by 12" deep. Total size with cornice and base is 34" wide, 14" deep at top, 55½" high, **$550-650.**

Taboret (plant stand), scalloped top and legs, top 11½" square, 15" high, **$55-75.**

Parlor table, incised lines on apron, top 24″ square, 28½″ high, **$115-145.**

Cylinder secretary, carved cornice and doors, 38″ wide, 22″ deep, 85″ high, **$1,750-1,950.**

Library table, curved apron, lyre-type legs, claw feet, 45″ wide, 26″ deep, 20″ high, **$575-675.**

Petite rolltop desk, wooden drawer handles, 36″ wide, 27½″ deep, 44″ high, **$750-850.**

Bookcase-desk combination, face carving on drop lid, bevel mirror, 39″ wide, 13½″ deep, 66½″ high, **$550-675.**

Divan (love seat), floral crest, 36″ wide, 20″ deep, 38½″ high, **$300-375.**

Hall bench, lift-lid for storage, cherry and oak combination, 35½″ wide, 19½″ deep, 38½″ high, **$350-425.**

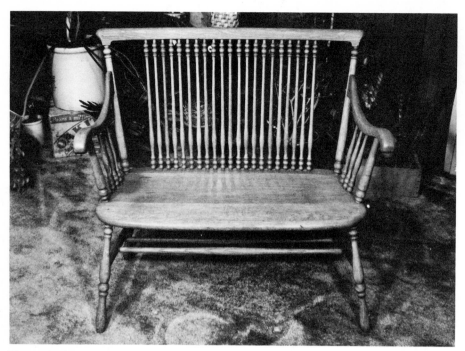

Unusual, dainty Windsor-type bench, splayed legs, H stretcher, 39″ wide, 16½″ deep, 35½″ high, **$350-450.**

Pressed back rocker, cane seat, 25″ arm to arm, 36″ high, **$185-235.**

Pressed back rocker, cane seat, 41″ high, **$135-160.**

Pressed back rocker, plank seat, Man of the North Wind design, 39″ high, **$175-200.**

Rocker, pressed design on lower slat, 25″ arm to arm, 33″ high, **$135-160.**

Unusual child's rocker, veneer back, seat was probably once veneered, 14½″ arm to arm, 25″ high, **$65-85.**

This chair is not oak, but oak chairs were made in this style. Gargoyle design, plank seat, H stretcher, 21″ arm to arm, 36½″ high, **$195-225.**

Parlor chair, pressed design on lower slats, slightly splayed legs, H stretcher, 25″ arm to arm, 39″ high, **$135-160.**

Round-seat chair with gentle cabriole legs. Bentwood hoop stretcher pierces front legs, 21½″ wide, 29½″ high, **$185-225.**

Taboret (plant stand), keyhole design in legs, top 12″ square, 19″ high, **$55-75.**

Taboret, six-sided, Oriental feel, top 13½″, 21″ high, **$125-165.**

Parlor table, scalloped top and shelf, reeded splayed legs, top 24″ square, 30″ high, **$95-125.**

Plant stand, round top and shelf, 16″ diameter, 18″ high, **$55-75.**

Parlor table, cabriole-type legs, top 24″ square, 30″ high, **$110-135.**

Parlor table, splayed legs, top 17½″ square, 30″ high, **$85-110.**

Parlor table, scalloped top and shelf. Shelf attached to legs with metal brackets, twist-turned legs, top 23″ square, 29″ high, **$125-145.**

Parlor table, curved apron, top, and shelf, cabriole legs, top 24″ square, 29½″ high, **$105-130.**

Parlor table, scalloped top and shelf, turned legs, 30″ wide, 22″ deep, 29″ high, **$85-115.**

Parlor table with drawer and shelf, unusual twist and spool turned legs, 34″ wide, 22″ deep, 27¾″ high, **$185-225.**

Parlor table with drawer, cabriole legs, 29″ wide, 22″ deep, 29″ high, **$165-195.**

Parlor table, circle beading on apron, scalloped shelf, top 24″ square, 28½″ high, **$115-135.**

Library table, ball and spindle construction, drawer in apron, 34″ wide, 28″ deep, 30″ high, **$455-555.**

Library table, heavy apron includes handleless drawer, pillar legs, 35″ wide, 26″ deep, 29″ high, **$145-175.**

Oval library table, handleless drawer, pillar legs, 38″ wide, 24″ deep, 30″ high, **$160-195.**

Table desk with drawer in apron, lyre-type legs. Families often associate an heirloom with the person who used it or the purpose for which it was used. To the owners, this is "Grandpa's desk," and many sermons were written as he worked there, 42″ wide, 26″ deep, 29″ high, **$175-225.**

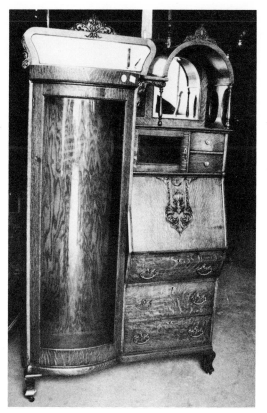

Bookcase-desk combination, convex (swell) glass, drop lid, applied carvings, 42″ wide, 13″ deep, 76″ high. Shop price, **$1,850.**

Lady's desk, drop lid, 26½″ wide, 16½″ deep, 46″ high, **$210-265.**

Desk, drop lid, replaced hardware, pressed designs, 21¾″ wide, 14″ deep, 41″ high, **$225-275.**

Lady's desk, drop lid, applied carving, 25½″ wide, 12″ deep, 41½″ high, **$225-325.**

Drop-lid desk, convex front drawers, 30″ wide, 16½″ deep, 49½″ high, **$275-350.**

Bookcase with adjustable shelves used for storing china, 39″ wide, 13½″ deep, 56½″ high, **$275-350.**

Bookcase, plain lines, 44″ wide, 12½″ deep, 52½″ high, **$300-375.**

Bookcase, leaded glass in 11″ high top section. Other sections 13½″ high. Glass doors pull up and slide in, 34″ wide, 12″ deep, 65½″ high. Label reads "Gunn Sectional Bookcase, pat. Dec. 5, 1899; June 1, 1901, Grand Rapids," originally finished in fumed oak, **$725-825.**

Bookcase in three stacked sections with doors which pull up and slide in. Sections 11″ high. Total size 34″ wide, 13″ deep, 42½″ high (used for goblet collection), **$450-525.**

Music cabinet, used to store sheet music, records, player piano rolls, 18″ wide, 16″ deep, 34″ high, **$110-135.**

Liquor cabinet with lock, no handle. Door with shelves for bottles swings out, scroll legs, 20″ wide, 16½″ deep, 34″ high, **$155-175.**

Take a chamber stick (a saucerlike candleholder with a fingerhold loop) or a kerosene lamp and ascend the stairs. Since bathrooms were not common in the early 1900s, and a back path led to the necessary building outdoors, the bedchamber needed nighttime accommodations. A potty with a lid peeked shyly out from under the bed, ready if required. A commode with its combination of drawers and doors could have a towel bar on top. Hidden within this piece was the lidded slop jar into which wastes were dumped to be carried out. A washbowl and large pitcher sat primly on top along with other parts of the chamber set such as a toothbrush holder, lidded soap dish, and a smaller pitcher. Hot and cold water were not delivered by pipes through a faucet. Instead, people carried water to their

Washstand commode, serpentine front, towel bar rail, 33″ wide, 19″ deep, 55½″ high, **$225-275.**

Towel bar washstand (mixed woods, including oak), porcelain knob on drawer, 23″ wide, 15″ deep, 22″ high, **$275-325.**

rooms in a pitcher. Woe be unto anyone who left water in a ceramic receptacle on a crisp winter night. By morning it might be ice-covered in the unheated bedchamber. Small washstands with one drawer and a shelf plus towel bar ends were manufactured in oak or other woods. These served as inexpensive chamber-set holders.

The chamber suite itself included a bedstand and dresser, often with an attached, swinging looking glass known as a cheval mirror. A high chest of drawers was listed as a chiffonier. A chest with space for hooks to hang garments was called a chifforobe. A wardrobe contained shelves plus hooks for hanging clothes, since built-in closets generally were a feature of the future.

Bed, applied decorations on headboard, posts, and crest, 59″ wide, 78½″ long, 60″ high, **$425-475.**

Cheval dresser, hat cabinet, applied carving, 42″ wide, 20½″ deep, 76″ high, **$450-525.**

Wardrobe, wood panels removed and glass inserted, functions as a china cabinet, applied carvings, 48″ wide, 18″ deep, 96″ high, **$725-825.**

Chiffonier, projecting parallel drawers, scroll feet, 32½″ wide, 19″ deep, 71″ high, **$225-275.**

Bed, applied decorations with carved leaves. Rails have been extended 8″, 57″ wide, 84″ long, foot 37″ high, headboard 57″ high, **$425-475.**

Single bed, applied carved decorations, 40″ wide, 76″ long, **$275-375.**

Bureau commode, plain lines, buttons on stiles, 38½″ wide, 19″ deep, 41″ high, **$225-275.**

Washstand commode, applied carvings, pressed-brass bail handles, 33″ wide, 18″ deep, 27″ high, **$135-175.**

Washstand commode, projection drawer, 34″ wide, 20″ deep, 28½″ high, **$135-175.**

Washstand commode, plain lines, pressed-brass bail handles, 30″ wide, 17½″ deep, 28″ high, **$135-175.**

Washstand commode, incised flowers on stiles, 30″ wide, 16″ deep, 27½″ high, **$260-315.**

Washstand commode, cast brass handles, plain lines, 32″ wide, 18″ deep, 29½″ high, **$165-195.**

Washstand commode, incised lines, pressed-brass bail handles, 29½″ wide, 16½″ deep, 29¼″ high, **$135-175.**

Washstand commode, cast brass bail handles, towel bar removed but available, 33" wide, 17" deep, 26" high, **$150-200.**

Washstand commode, towel bar top, replaced handles, 36" wide, 19" deep, 44" high, **$225-275.**

Washstand commode with towel bar, serpentine projection front, 34" wide, 20" deep, 53" high, **$235-285.**

Dresser, three plain drawers with wooden pulls, 38″ wide, 17½″ deep, 32″ high, **$125-165.**

Dresser on high straight legs, 38″ wide, 19″ deep, 27″ high, **$135-165.**

Dresser, three plain drawers with wooden pulls, scalloped top, 36″ wide, 17½″ deep, 33″ high, **$125-165.**

Dresser, serpentine projection front, beading on straight apron, paper label reads "West Michigan Furniture Co., Holland, Mich.," 21″ wide, 41½″ deep, 33″ high, **$135-175.**

Dresser, serpentine front, including apron, 42″ wide, 21″ deep, 35″ high, **$135-175.**

Dresser, veneered serpentine front, cabriole legs, 36″ wide, 20″ deep, 28″ high, **$125-155.**

Dresser, scalloped projection top, parallel drawers, 45½″ wide, 22½″ deep, 33″ high, **$145-175.**

Dresser, mirror replaced, three parallel drawers with middle drawer swelling and projecting, high legs, 42″ wide, 20″ deep, 65″ high, **$225-275.**

Dresser, applied carvings on swinging mirror frame, two parallel drawers, projecting high legs, 40″ wide, 18½″ deep, 69½″ high, **$250-350.**

Dresser, serpentine front, scalloped apron, 41″ wide, 19″ deep, 72″ high, **$275-375.**

Ornate dresser, serpentine front, including apron, floral crest on center mirror, side looking glasses are adjustable, 42″ wide, 22″ deep, 73″ high, **$300-375.**

Washstand commode, serpentine projection front, turned posts support swinging mirror, 31½″ wide, 18″ deep, 52″ high, **$200-275.**

Dresser, pronounced quarter-sawed oak, 42″ wide, 21″ deep, 68½″ high, **$195-295.**

Dresser, applied carvings, including crest above swinging mirror, 44″ wide, 22″ deep, 75½″ high, **$250-350.**

Dresser, serpentine front, including apron, round pilaster above swinging mirror, applied carvings, 42″ wide, 20″ deep, 77″ high, **$275-375.**

Dresser, called a "princess dresser" by owner, applied crest on mirror frame, beading on apron, 41″ wide, 21″ deep, 73″ high, **$325-395.**

Chiffonier, ornate cast brass hardware, 35″ wide, 17½″ deep, 50″ high, **$250-300.**

Chiffonier, incised lines, 33″ wide, 18″ deep, 41″ high, **$250-300.**

Chiffonier, serpentine front, wooden pulls, 30″ wide, 19″ deep, 40″ high, **$225-275.**

Chiffonier, two parallel serpentine drawers projecting, scalloped apron, high legs, 33¼″ wide, 18″ deep, 54¼″ high, **$225-275.**

Chiffonier, unusual top includes hat cabinet, pilasters between parallel drawers, serpentine projection front, claw feet, 42″ wide, 22″ deep, 46½″ high, **$245-295.**

Chiffonier with swinging mirror, applied crest, 28″ wide, 16½″ deep, 54½″ high, **$235-285.**

Wardrobe, molded cornice, applied carving, 44″ wide, 16½″ deep, 80″ high, **$425-525.**

Wardrobe, comes apart for ease in transporting, two panels on doors have arched tops, molded cornice, 48″ wide, 17″ deep, 80″ high, **$425-525.**

Wardrobe, ornate incised carving, 44″ wide, 16″ deep, 81½″ high, **$325-425.**

Wardrobe, incised carving on cornice, 39″ wide, 16″ deep, 80″ high, **$375-475.**

Wardrobe, beading and applied carving on cornice, 44″ wide, 19″ deep, 80¼″ high, **$325-425.**

Some authorities place golden oak after Mission oak, but the gold finish was actually advertised ten years prior to the time Gustav Stickley first publicly showed his "Craftsman" furniture in 1900. The gold comes in first. It ran alongside Mission and emerged afterwards. Like General MacArthur's old soldier story, styles do not die, they simply fade away. While one is waning, another is rising to replace it. The two may blend for a time, the new retaining some aspects of the old, so that there is a transitional stage, not an abrupt rupture. By the 1930s walnut or mahogany veneer furniture was established, and golden oak was all but gone. It would return another day.

Rolltop desk, S roll, right side of base has one drawer and a file door, 48″ wide, 31″ deep, 48″ high. Shop price, **$1,950.**

Rolltop desk, beading on top, fan-shaped drawer pulls, brass metal tags for inner files, 64½″ wide, 36″ deep, 49½″ high. Shop price, **$6,800.**

This unusual rolltop desk has another roll on the left side of the kneehole with a pullout shelf, 55″ wide, 34″ deep, 52½″ high. Shop price, **$2,300.**

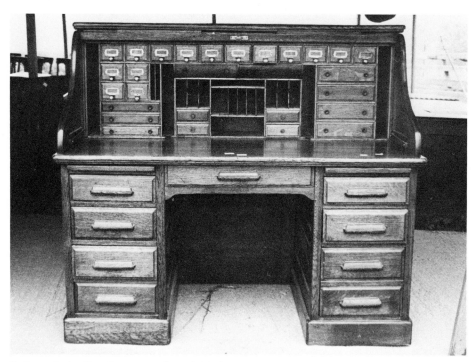

Rolltop desk, S roll, patent date 1884, brass metal tags for inner files, finished back, 59½″ wide, 33½″ deep, 51″ high. Shop price, **$5,750.**

Swivel desk chair, pressed cane seat, 22″ arm to arm, 40½″ high, **$225-275.**

Swivel desk chair, mixed woods, mostly ash, cane seat, 21½″ arm to arm, 43″ high, **$250-300.**

Pressed back swivel desk chair, cane seat, 22″ arm to arm, 42″ high, **$275-350.**

Game table, late 1880s, cabriole legs, bottom shelf is concave on all sides to allow for leg room. Top removed shows spinning pointers for game, 32″ square, 29″ high, **$550-650.**

Game table in closed position.

4 Painted or Changed— It's Still Oak

People often ask, "What was the original factory finish on Hoosier cabinets?" Perusing old magazines, newspapers, and catalogs (or catalogues, as it used to be spelled) helps dredge up the past and filter out the facts. It seems a white or gray surface, exterior as well as interior, was prominent, although a golden oak finish was also offered. That original enamel adhered tighter than a skirt with static electricity clings to nylon hose. Try to remove it, and it's most uncooperative.

Hoosier cabinets were made in New Castle, Indiana, the Hoosier state. Although various firms offered a similar product with other monikers, this name clung as tenaciously as a stick-me-tight seed to a pair of slacks. These cupboards thus acquired their generic title.

Research readily shows the evolution of the simple kitchen work table into what was to become the Hoosier cabinet. A table with drawers and a flour or meal bin

Hoosier-type cabinet, circa 1930s, white factory finish, label reads "Ingram Richardson Mfg. Co., Frankfort, Ind." Porcelain pullout top, rolltop door, 40" wide, 25" deep, 70¼" high, **$225-350.**

seems to have come first. (Some people call this a baker's table, today.) Later, a discerning individual must have considered the top wasted space and added shelves above. Built-in flour sifters and sugar containers, condiment jars, and a sliding metal or porcelain top that provided a more spacious work surface were subsequently added. Special models sparkled with colored glass panels to add beauty.

By the ads, it appears that a housewife who received a Hoosier or a facsimile would have (Sears said) "The Happiest Surprise of Her Life." The Sears 1927 Catalog offered a Hoosier in golden oak, white, or gray enamel. Naturally, it had to be a masculine ad writer who envisioned the service a cupboard could give. Would you enjoy a meal prepared and tidied up afterward by a cabinet? The copy almost implied such assistance. "Let it work for you in your home as you pay for it." It cost $39.95 in oak, obtainable for five dollars down and five dollars monthly, plus a small installment fee. Painted finishes cost a little more. This deluxe edition included bill, coin, sugar, flour, meal, recipe (receipt), dish, pan, bread, and grocery holders; plus menu planners and weights and measures charts. It must have been quite a convenience to have all these necessities available in one location.

Hoosier-type cabinet, three colored glass panels, rolltop door, flour sifter, label reads "Sellers The Better Kitchen Cabinet Kitchen Maid, Elwood, Ind., U.S.A. Trademark registered," 40½" wide, 26½" deep, 69½" high. Shop price, **$750.**

Hoosier-type cabinet used as all-in-one unit for baby. Quilted pad over pullout porcelain top for diaper changing, diapers kept in flour bin, drawers for clothes, 40″ wide, 27″ deep, extends to 37″ pulled out, 68½″ high, **$350-450.**

A modern young homemaker uses imagination to make her kitchen cabinet of yore serve well. She can pad the pullout top and have a just-the-right-height surface for diapering the baby.

While no advertiser dreamed up that usage, sellers felt it was a great creation. A sales pitch from the June 21, 1910, issue of the Madison *Daily Herald*, published in Madison, Indiana, was quoted in our book *Country Pine Furniture Styles and Prices* and is worth repeating. It woos buyers in this manner: "Wife needs a helper with the work; you can't get a good girl, you've tried it; listen, here's a secret: it's just like play with a HOOSIER KITCHEN CABINET. You don't have to feed it, or house it, or teach it, or wage it or beau it. The Hoosier is it; everything handy, ready to use;…saves time, saves expenses…. Don't wait to be coaxed, get it for her now." It was available at Vail's. Who could resist such an appeal?

Hoosier cabinet made in New Castle, Ind., "The Hoosier Saves Steps" in oval, zinc top, 42″ wide, 25″ deep, 71″ high, **$375-425.**

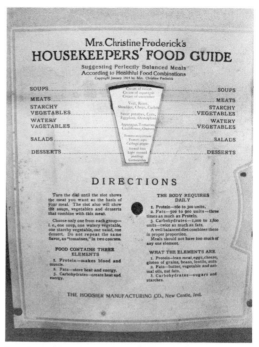

Food guide inside cabinet still intact.

Hoosier-type cabinet, top has breadboard ends, pullout cutting board, 40″ wide, 24″ deep, 69″ high, **$375-425.**

Hoosier cabinet, hardware marked "Feb. 10, 1910 Hoosier," pullout wooden top, bread box, flour sifter, 30″ wide, 24″ deep, 66½″ high, **$275-350.**

Hoosier-type cabinet, called "June Bride," manufactured by Sellers, replaced drawer knobs, pull-out porcelain shelf, metal bread box, sifter, 40½" wide, 25" deep, 70" high, **$475-575.**

China cabinet, sides and doors convex glass, claw feet, carefully antiqued by the owners to produce a delightful appearance, 42" wide, 14" deep, 66" high, **$600-675.**

There are those who are quick to slap on paint. Sometimes when people do not like fumed oak and are unable to remove this seeped-in darkness from the large, open pores, they resort to paint. A process referred to as "antiquing" is frequently done by applying a light base and highlighting with a deeper hue. This can produce attractive results, especially when the predominate color in the room is picked up.

There are also cutdowns. A cutdown today is usually interpreted to mean a barbed, ego-shattering remark. In a similar manner, a cutdown can be just as harmful to furniture values. While, antiquewise, it is not recommended that furniture undergo major surgery, some people find that cutdowns can be extremely functional. One serviceable form is a round oak pedestal dining room table converted into a coffee table by slashing out part of the pillar. These are comments which show how some owners feel about the results. "Frankly, we like it in front of our sofa. You can't hurt it. We can prop our feet on it to relax. We can throw pillows on the floor and flop down to play cards or to write letters. We can have trays and watch a TV ballgame while we eat. You can't imagine how much we use it." Another states, "It's just the right size for our children to read, play, or eat at." Library tables can receive a similar cutting treatment to fill a like need.

Library table cut to coffee table height, drawer in apron, thick round pillar legs, scrolled feet, 42" wide, 26" deep, 18" high, **$275-375.**

Hat cabinet removed from a cheval dresser, now used as a bedside stand, applied carving on door, 14" wide, 13" deep, 35" high, **$75-100.**

The term "cheval," spelled "chevalle" in original ads, is derived from the French word meaning "horse." Just as a horse supports its rider, in the same way, an outer frame surrounds a cheval mirror to provide the stable support for the swinging looking glass. The hat cabinet beside the mirror is sometimes sliced off the chest and used as a small stand, with its drawers and door proving convenient for that purpose.

Spool cabinet, lift-lid desk for store counter, J. & P. Coats thread, on a sewing machine metal base to form a self-standing desk, 30″ wide, 21″ deep, 12″ high, **$375-425.**

Another piece which often goes through the surgical process is the old-fashioned treadle sewing machine. The drawers can be secured together with a top and thus be converted into a petite stand. The metal base becomes handsome legs for a table with a top of marble, wood, or glass. As mentioned earlier, a marriage occurs when unrelated individual items are joined together to form a different piece of furniture. An intricate sewing machine base may be topped with a lift-lid, counter-top spool cabinet. A self-supporting desk is the child of this union.

Sewing machines of yore don't have to be cutups. Why not electrify grandma's oldster so that it can serve the new generation? If the lines and designs on a passé case are pleasing, the unit might form a small, decorative table—a conversation piece in an otherwise blah room.

Singer sewing machine, electrified, currently in use, 35½″ wide, 17″ deep, 30½″ high, **$55-75.**

Ornate sewing machine with beading and pressed designs, Wheeler & Wilson Mfg. Co., Bridgeport, Conn., March 25, 1890 last patent date, top 33" x 16", **$75-125.**

Singer sewing machine with beading, carving, and brightly painted machine head, July 21, 1903, latest patent, top 36" x 18", **$75-100.**

This sewing machine cabinet resembles a desk. Lift lid to pull up machine head. Two doors open to hold sewing accessories in wooden bin inserts, beading, incised lines, 24" wide, 22" deep, 34" high, **$225-275.**

Singer sewing machine, incised lines on drawers, ornate painting on machine head, top 36" x 18", **$45-65.**

Speaking of conversational pieces brings to mind the telephone. Ringing up Central (the operator) by turning the crank on a phone could arouse everyone on the party line to listen in on the ensuing discussion between the caller and the callee. That was the day when you might turn out a number by cranking one long and two short rings or other combinations to get the person you wanted.

For a long time telephones were gutted to create spice racks or to house radios, but now people enjoy them intact. Sometimes they become intercoms in a home, or the telephone company can be requested to connect them properly so that they are functional once more.

Kellogg telephone, complete, brass replated, 11" wide, 25" high, **$175-225.**

Telephone manufactured by Eureka Electric Co., Chicago, 12" wide, 32" high. Shop price, **$345.**

This label found in an oak wardrobe advertises Shallene Bros. furniture dealers, Moline, Ill. Save labels whenever possible.

The pointer pictured on this page is not included to urge you to patronize a now defunct store. Instead, it is a reminder: Whenever you are able, save that label! Besides engendering interest, labels help to identify and date a piece and therefore may increase its value. For example, a label could have nostalgic appeal in the area mentioned, or a recognized quality craftsman or designer may be indicated. Hubbard, Larkin, Roycrofter, and Stickley come to mind immediately when the word "oak" is uttered. Their names cause the price thermometer to register higher. (This pointer was found inside a wardrobe which was not positioned so that it could be photographed well.)

Wouldn't past generations be surprised to see how occupational castoffs are incorporated into modern decors? Spool cabinets once given away as free display

Spool cabinet, Richardsons, ten glass front drawers, one made of wood, 19½" square, 25" high, **$350-450.**

Label found on back of spool cabinet reads "Richardsons Perfect Silk."

cases to storekeepers no longer hold thread for the home seamstress but are reincarnated as tables in homey environments. Now that's a transition! Boxes with advertisements on them are recycled. Store showcases are rejuvenated and become china display or hobby centers, and barbers' cabinets now hang on walls in the home. A machinist chest may sit on milady's dresser and hold accessory articles such as jewelry, belts, and scarfs. Imagination—that's what it takes to decorate with discarded items. It'll take lots of creative power and plenty of space to adapt a six-foot long Siamese twin back-to-back double bench from a railroad waiting room to home living quarters. With all the emphasis on train lore, perhaps someone will adopt the unique bench pictured here.

Railroad waiting room bench, back-to-back double seat, flower medallion above legs, pressed wood back and seat, patterns formed with pierced holes, 72″ long, **$450-550.**

Label found on the back of the cabinet.

Spool cabinet counter desk, J. & P. Coats, hole for inkwell in top gallery, leather writing insert. Supplied to storekeeper as an advertisement. Store accounts were kept inside the lift-lid, **$375-425.**

Round spool cabinet, Merrick's Six Cord, patented July 20, 1897. Thread was inserted in a hole in the top and removed at the base. The knob rotates the spool holder, 18″ diameter, 19¾″ high, **$475-575.**

Spool cabinet, Corticelli Silk and Twist, twenty-six glass front drawers, four wooden drawers, brass pulls, 44½″ wide, 18″ deep, 43″ high, **$1,250-1,350.**

Display cabinet from store, 22½″ wide, 23½″ deep at base, tapers to 13½″ at top, 49″ high, **$325-425.**

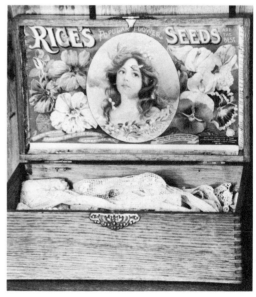

Box, "Rice's Popular Flower Seeds Are The Best, Cambridge Valley Seed Gardens, Cambridge, N.Y.," 11″ wide, 6½″ deep, 4″ high, **$55-75.**

Machinist chest, label reads, "Union, the Chest Co., Inc., Rochester, N.Y.," bottom pulls out to enclose drawers. Leather handle for ease in transporting. Currently used for jewelry, scarfs, belts, and sundries, 20″ wide, 8″ deep, 13″ high, **$95-110.**

Tool cabinet, large hinges, closes for carrying, 31″ wide, 5¾″ deep, 17″ high, **$55-85.**

Type cabinet, manufactured by the Hamilton Mfg. Co., Two Rivers, Wis. Handles stamped "Hamilton Mfg. Co.," 37″ wide, 22″ deep, 43″ high, **$675-775.**

File box, four drawers, 13″ wide, 15½″ deep, 9″ high, **$55-75.**

Tavern table with four compartments to hold beverages. Top surface remains free for playing cards, 40″ wide, 29½″ deep, 31″ high, **$350-400.**

Either a store counter or probably a library case as it has an inventory number on a metal tag. Glass door remains open, straight legs, base and molded top come off to form three sections, 34″ wide, 12″ deep, 25½″ high, **$125-150.**

Box for holding sick call set for the home, Roman Catholic, two metal candleholders; supplies kept inside drop lid, 13½″ wide, 24″ high, **$65-85.**

Barber cabinet, two drawers, drop-down drawer, incised lines, brass hardware, open shelf in base, 24″ wide, 13½″ deep, 36″ high, **$425-475.**

Barber cabinet, two doors, drop-lid compartment beneath, 16¼″ wide, 9¼″ deep, 19″ high, **$110-145.**

Combination china cabinet-cupboard with burled highlights and leaded glass in center pane, 59½" wide, 19" deep, 89" high, **$1,350-1,500.**

Bed with applied decorations, 58″ wide, 78½″ long, 63″ high overall dimensions, **$450-500.** Three-drawer chest at foot of bed, 38″ wide, 18″ deep, 25″ high, **$135-165.**

Chiffonier with serpentine projecting drawer and attached mirror, 32″ wide, 20″ deep, 69½″ high, **$250-325.**

Mixed-woods towel bar washstand commode, 31″ wide, 17″ deep, 68″ high, **$225-300.**

Ash secretary with walnut handles and decorations, 41″ wide, 19″ deep, 88″ high, **$1,500-1,750.**

Built-in leaded glass cabinet, 31″ wide, 59″ high, **$525-600.**

China cabinet with muntins, turned legs, mirror behind top shelf, 37½″ wide, 15″ deep, 61½″ high, **$475-575.**

Hoosier-type kitchen cupboard, 40″ wide, 25″ deep, 70″ high, **$625-725.**

Round pedestal table, 45″ diameter, **$500-600.** Plate rail, **$65-95.** Two pressed back chairs with pressed cane seat, **$115-145 each.** High chair, **$125-165.**

Child's rocker with pressed cane seat, 12″ to seat, 29½″ high, **$135-165.**

Kitchen cabinet, projecting top drawers and sunken door panels, 38″ wide, 20½″ deep, 80½″ high, **$375-475.**

Cupboard with flower and leaf carvings on each of four doors, 41″ wide, 18″ deep, 74½″ high, **$550-650.**

Drop-leaf extension table, 41″ wide, 24″ deep, 29½″ high, **$225-275.**

Bed lounge, folds out, sleeps two, 72″ wide, 24″ deep, 38″ high, **$750-850.**

5 The Arts and Crafts Movement

Ruskin, Eastlake, Morris, Stickley, Hubbard—rebels, that's what they were. With harsh swift hands these men, who emphasized craftmanship, brushed away shoddy machine workmanship, and late Victorian clutter, curves, and eclecticism. Home was to be the place where quiet, peaceful, practical designs should prevail, blending as smoothly as a disco skater blends with the rollers on his feet.

This was not a newborn concept. Back in the late 1700s, England's architect brothers, Robert and James Adam, promoted a beautiful but sterile union of architecture and furnishings in which everything was compatible. Even mirrors and wall hangings had assigned stations in the elegant design and were to remain there constantly. Consoles and statues were given permanent niches. Floors reflected the same swags and medallion motifs as did the ceiling above. Homeyness was forgotten in a perfection of pattern that coordinated all precisely.

In the latter half of the 1800s, yet another group accepted this idea of oneness. Men who followed this cult challenged the establishment. Ruskin believed all work should pass three tests. Is it honest, useful, and cheerful? Morris stated that "Real art is the expression by man of his pleasure in labor." They believed that only the useful and beautiful should be in a home, and neither price nor fashion should determine art or quality. A dedication to hand workmanship was sought by members of the British Art Workers Guild. Interior designs, glass, jewelry, printing, ceramics, architecture, and furniture were all influenced by this new expression. To the promoters, their nectar was personal individual achievement in the crafts, even if results were a wee bit quaint and crude. They ignored the fact that machines made many products available to the rising middle-class purchaser that formerly had only been within the means of those with higher incomes. The movement's detractors realized that machines could not be snapped off like beans from a stalk. They were needed and not to be disregarded. The movement was not greeted with delight by the masses.

Was it a London-born social reformer, writer, art critic, and Oxford professor who was the granddaddy of the English Arts and Crafts Movement which spread to continental Europe as well as, in some degree, to the United States? This man, affluent John Ruskin (1819-1900), at least deserves a portion of the credit. Perhaps because he was acquainted with Biblical teachings, he supported social reforms and spent much of his inheritance improving the conditions of the working class.

Ruskin felt that good architecture was related to moral feeling and therefore was religious in tone. Some authorities think Ruskin's discussions did help foster change.

Another rebel felt that cheap and slipshod work often resulted from the rapid

Lady's desk, drop lid, incised carving and lines, brass pulls, 29" wide, 16" deep, 59½" high, **$475-575.**

machines, but he was not opposed to their contributions and usage. Straight is strong. Simple is striking. Box it up. These were three concepts belonging to this man, England's Charles Lock Eastlake (1836-1906). He might well have believed in the geometric principle that the shortest distance between two points is a straight line, for he maintained that round designs wasted wood. His book, *Hints on Household Taste*, published around 1868, promoted rectangles and squares. Chip carving and incised parallel lines (now sometimes referred to as railroad tracks) were attractive decorative touches that did not recklessly use extra wood. Eastlake opposed the marketing of inferior commercial wares which were turned out too rapidly by some factories where proper design was heedlessly ignored. His mass-production-oriented predecessors and contemporaries were apparently so delighted with the ability of their power driven machines that they borrowed, adopted, and combined any patterns from the past that pleased them. Eastlake found this eclectic tendency disturbing. His uncluttered designs crossed the Atlantic and settled in the United States around 1870, retaining their hold on fashion until about

Rectangular parlor table, Eastlake influence, incised carving, 31½" wide, 22" deep, 27½" high, **$155-195.**

1890. While Eastlake and his devotees in England tended to use oak or ash, walnut was still the number one wood in America, although it was waning both in popularity and availability.

The industry did accept Eastlake's rectilinear plans. Designers were hired to go creative, and what some of them did to his box was astounding. So many appendages and doodads were added that the resulting products did not have the simple look Eastlake advocated. He liked the clean, practical, functional Japanese furniture, or the touches of steeples and tracery borrowed from the old Gothic. How he must have shuddered at the overexuberance with which his peers espoused his ideas, adding excessive curlicues to his Quakerish plainness. Although it was difficult to discard all the frills immediately, the industry was ready for a change and wanted to promote conscious designing. Thus England's Charles Lock Eastlake did foster a new trend where curves were out of style and going straight was fashionable.

Washstand commode, incised carving, incised lines, Eastlake style, 32″ wide, 18½″ deep, 36″ high, **$275-325.**

Washstand commode, incised carving and lines, Eastlake, 30″ wide, 16½″ deep, 30″ high, **$245-295.** *Painting by Anne Ross from a photograph in National Geographic.*

Washstand commode, marble top added, replaced handles, incised lines, Eastlake, 32″ wide, 17″ deep, 34″ high, **$350-450.**

116

Dresser, hardware replaced with glass knobs, incised carving and lines, Eastlake, 40″ wide, 18″ deep, 31½″ high, **$150-200.**

Eastlake parlor table, 29″ wide, 21½″ deep, 29″ high, **$165-195.**

Washstand commode, marble top added, Eastlake, incised designs and lines, 32″ wide, 18″ deep, 28″ high, **$350-450.**

Pedestal parlor table, 25″ wide, 20″ deep, 29″ high, **$95-135.**

Wardrobe changed to china cabinet by removing wooden panels and substituting glass, 40″ wide, 15½″ deep, 77½″ high, **$475-575.**

Wardrobe, beveled glass, pillars on stiles, 55″ wide, 20″ deep, 87½″ high, **$1,250-1,350.**

Eastlake cane chair, set of 4, **$75-95, each.**

Bookcase, plank sides, carved cornice. Original owner purchased this with his first month's pay as a schoolteacher, 42″ wide, 11½″ deep, 80½″ high, **$950-1,150.**

Oak organ, 41″ wide, 23″ deep, 75″ high. No price available at owner's request.

Morris-type armchair recliner with elaborate carving on rolled arms and front supports, 28″ arm to arm, 39″ high, **$275-375.**

Morris chair, pins and hinges regulate height, drawer at base, 27½″ arm to arm, 39″ high, **$165-195.**

Another socialistically inclined leader of the English Arts and Crafts Movement, poet William Morris (1834-1896), was an interior designer who advocated the return to excellence in total craftmanship. Since he delved into church history as a college student, it was fitting that he helped establish a company that specialized in ecclesiastical furnishings. Wood carvings, embroidery, tapestries, stained glass windows, murals, and mosaics were produced, until, as the business expanded, it served secular interests as well. Wallpaper, furniture, and carpets received his attention, but to the average man this poet is probably most commonly associated with the invention of the Morris chair—the chair which permitted reclining. The upholstered back could be slanted at various angles. A movable rod placed in the desired groove retained the proper incline for one's comfort.

The next cultural revolutionary, Gustav Stickley (1857-1942), is credited with developing a new style of furniture, a United States special. Its lines remind one of Morris's functional recliner with its uncluttered look. Perhaps Stickley was under William Morris's sphere of influence.

Who was Gustav Stickley? If you had asked him, he would have told you he was the creator of THE UNIQUE Craftsman furniture. All other staunch, straight-lined, strong oak examples were copies that could not compare, he would have said. He disliked these imitations and was not flattered that furniture makers emulated his work. This multifaceted man was a writer, designer, manufacturer, editor, and home builder who developed squat bungalow houses which contrasted with the wood-wasting tall edifices which might be their neighbors. These smaller homes were inexpensive and provided the "just right" setting for his functional Craftsman furnishings. Such coordination of exterior and interior designs was a key theme of the Arts and Crafts Movement. With the passage of years, the Stickley-copyrighted Craftsman name was swallowed up by another title which distressed and disturbed this builder. The generic term used by competitors who fashioned their furniture after his was "Mission," the name currently assigned to this style. Stickley, bungalows, and Mission furniture are discussed in more detail later.

Mission rocker, 26½" arm to arm, 32" high, **$85-125.**

Another dissident in the United States was Elbert Hubbard (1856-1915), who led his army of dissenters to establish a craft colony at East Aurora, New York. Just as Brigham Young guided the Mormans westward to settle, irrigate, and reclaim the dry wasteland in Utah, so did Hubbard inspire and nourish handmade artistry in a mechanized wasteland.

This peaceful revolutionary worked for a time with his brother-in-law, John D. Larkin. The latter started a company using his name in 1875. By 1892, the company became the Larkin Soap Manufacturing Company. Hubbard was a published writer and a skilled advertising agent who helped develop the "Larkin Club" for housewives and their friends and relatives. Housewives were encouraged to join the Larkin Club, earning delightful premiums in exchange for purchases, thus creating an incentive to be Larkin loyalists. Years after Hubbard's demise, these groups remained in existence. The free, 1925 fiftieth anniversary catalog listed Larkin's alluring array of household products. Free gifts available as awards for

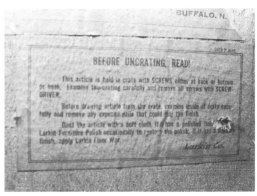

Label found on back of Larkin bookcase-desk combination.

Bookcase-desk combination supplied by Larkin Company, 42" wide, 14" deep, 67" high, **$1,250-1,450.**

promoting Larkin Clubs included "furniture, lamps, rugs, curtains, silverware, linens, and other lovely things for the home." Buffalo, New York, was the manufacturing location for Larkin furniture.

Elbert Hubbard left his brother-in-law's company after he visited England and came to accept William Morris's rejection of machines. By 1895, handicraft artisans who joined Hubbard's East Aurora Colony became known as "Roycrofters," and their products may be marked "Roycroft." They created pottery, leather articles, textiles, jewelry, metal objects, and they printed books. Their straight-lined, handmade furniture was in the Mission style, adapted from that designed by Gustav Stickley.

Then, suddenly, on May 7, 1915, a newspaper headline read, "Passenger Ship *Lusitania* Sunk by German Sub. 1,198 perish, including 128 Americans." Among those lost at sea was Elbert Hubbard. The Roycrofters had lost their leader. (Other accounts list 112 American victims.)

These are only a few of the men who felt the influence of the Arts and Crafts Movement. Many architects, artisans, builders, artists, and designers rejected overmechanization, finding it distasteful, and turned to the wholesome nourishment of creative hand craftmanship.

6 Craftsman—
Furniture with a Mission

What is hearsay and what is fact? There are conflicting reports as to how the native-to-America Mission furniture was conceived. Was it a derivative of the English Arts and Crafts Movement or was it religious in origin? Some say its roots are in the crude, straight-lined furnishings pounded together out of necessity by the noncarpenter, long-robed Spanish monks and their converted Indian parishioners who struggled to construct utilitarian seats and tables for their rustic churches in the old Southwest. This appealing tale would explain both the name and the austerity of the Mission style. As if to prove their religious ancestry some chairs and benches bear cutout crosses on their backs.

Library table with drawer exposure on both sides, 41" wide, 27" deep, 30" high, **$105-135.**

The 1908 *Sears, Roebuck Catalogue*, reprinted by The Gun Digest Company, displays a banner presenting "SPECIAL VALUES IN MISSION FURNITURE." It enthusiastically proclaims that this style is not an experiment, but after years of availability, retains its popularity. Prominent architects recommend the furnishings to clients since they blend together strength, comfort, beauty, and simplicity. The ad links secular commercialism with the religious by explaining that similar furnishings were found in Spanish missions in the Southwest, and designs based on their structure received the approval of the Arts and Crafts societies in both England and the United States.

Other authorities feel the name has a different origin. Furnishings have a purpose, or mission. A bed is for resting. A chair is for sitting. A table is to sit at or to hold items. Each item had its own reason for being, and thus was furniture with a mission. Still another explanation comes from George Grotz who writes with mirth and meaning in his informative books. He contends that Gustav Stickley wanted to coordinate architecture and furniture. In order to accomplish this unification he developed stoic Craftsman furnishings to complement the bungalows he designed and constructed. A promoter called these structures Spanish mission and the name stuck not only to the walls of the abodes but to the contents inside as well. Maybe all of these versions combine to explain Mission oak with its strength and strict simple lines.

Mission oak side chair, **$35-45.**

But who could explain Gustav Stickley? The man was an enigma. He renounced the furniture produced by his emulators in his magazine, *The Craftsman,* and also in his catalogs. As quickly as St. Nick could call out the names of his reindeer, Stickley crossed off his copiers. Avoid "Hand-Craft," "Mission," "Roycroft," "Quaint," "Arts and Crafts," and others, he said. But the most odious was "Stickley Furniture" produced by those who shared his family name. Why buy the shadow when the genuine article was available? (And naturally, of such superior quality.) Craftsman was the best, he contended.

Label found under oval folding table.

Stickley oval folding parlor table, spool legs, folds flat to store, label underneath reads "Quaint Furniture, Stickley Bros. Co., Grand Rapids, Mich.," 24″ wide, 18½″ deep, 24″ high, **$350-400.**

But, and here is the puzzlement, Gustav Stickley did not do what another designer did. John Belter (1795-1865) laminated rich woods such as rosewood, walnut, sometimes oak, then tortured, bent, and pierced them, ornately carving natural motifs. It is said this nineteenth century craftsman destroyed his designs to frustrate and deter copiers. Not Stickley. He believed in home do-it-yourself projects and encouraged amateurs to send for his designs so that they, too, could build quality furnishings inexpensively at home. His materials were available to those who sought to be creative. Customers could order leather, upholstery materials, metal trim, and plans with instructions. Fabrics which were stamped for needlework intrigued the ladies. Stickley felt that pleasing, well-designed, and well-executed furniture helped improve the moral fiber of a home. He did not like the senseless, overly ornamented furniture John Belter and his peers cherished. Sincere furnishings help shape honest men and women, according to Stickley's philosophy. Despite the fact that loss of sales might hurt him in the wallet, he spread the tenet of handmade furniture. The Arts and Crafts Movement influenced Gustav Stickley when he visited England and Europe, and he adopted some of their teachings. His attitude was: Commercial imitators—no! Home handymen—yes!

Mission library table, 42" wide, 25½" deep, 30¼" high, **$185-225.**

Mission one-drawer smoking stand, 12¼" wide, 10½" deep, 29½" high, **$90-115.**

Early in his life, this Wisconsin farm lad worked in furniture factories and stores learning about wood, construction, styles, and merchandising. This exposure fostered his dislike for the flimsy, fussy furnishings mass-produced in factories. In spite of this, from about 1880 to mid-1890, Stickley and his four brothers manufactured conventional, late Victorian furniture. The Stickley Brothers Company is mentioned in material at the Grand Rapids Public Library. A leaflet, "Furniture—The Product of Pride," stated that from 1880 to 1900 more than eighty-five furniture manufacturers started business in that city, including the Stickley Company.

Gustav Stickley wanted to improve the quality of furniture while reducing its cost. He opened a workshop in Eastwood, near Syracuse, New York, around 1895. By 1898 he was experimenting with plain, functional, solid, comfortable, durable, rectangular lines as his Craftsman ideas took their natal steps. Stickley didn't plan to develop a new furniture design, it just happened. His baby, Craftsman, became an integral part of his life, and he adopted almost a perfectionist attitude in his desire to create each piece well. Purchasers were encouraged to return any unsatisfactory pieces so the quality could be retained. His wood specialty was white oak, but he also used other indigenous varieties.

Wood requires a coating of some type to keep it from shrinking and swelling in the humidity and to keep it from absorbing dirt or acquiring stains. (For example, water that penetrates the wood leaves black spots such as the ringed outline from a damp glass or bowl.) A sealing agent also helps accentuate the character and beauty of the lumber used. Because of this, various finishes are applied to furniture. Stickley liked fumed oak because it resembled patina, the natural darkening of furniture with age, use, and exposure to light. To obtain this appearance, Craftsman articles were moistened to open the pores and placed in an air-tight compartment, usually for forty-eight hours, depending on the depth of color desired. Containers of strong ammonia provided the vapors that penetrated

Mission rocker, upholstered seat, 24" arm to arm, 34" high, **$90-115.**

Mission rocker, 24½" arm to arm, 35½" high, **$85-110.**

the wood, which later was meticulously hand sanded until smooth. Over that, Stickley applied his own special coating to achieve one of three tones — a soft silver gray, or a light or deep brown. Craftsman Wood Luster was rubbed on to complete the process so that his fumed oak furniture was armored for marketing.

Although purists usually want pieces left as found to preserve their value, some owners do not like this finish and have found it difficult to remove. One man exclaimed, "After I stripped the surface, I sanded for days and finally got it clean. It was a devil of a job!" Gustav Stickley was so proud of his workmanship that such treatment of one of his wooden offsprings might have made him angrily grit his teeth or clench his fists, but it was his own belief that furnishings should fit the home and provide comfort for the owners. If they said, "Let it be light," that would be their choice. The piece mentioned earlier was not a Stickley. But if it were, an owner should think twice before changing the finish, for many collectors would embrace the original fumed finish ecstatically.

Cushions were covered with genuine leather or sheepskin specially treated not to craze or check, and waterproofed to add endurance. Cheaper versions manufactured by other firms were made of artificial leather, but these were not fine enough to pass Stickley's standards for softness and beauty.

By 1900, he sought to share his bold, utilitarian lines with the world. He displayed samples of his original designs at the Furniture Exposition in Grand Rapids, Michigan. Visitors realized that Gustav Stickley had introduced a new, uncluttered furniture style. It was as American as the Indians' popcorn and a housewife's apple pie. Others seized upon his ideas and, with a few changes in design and titles, brought forth similar furniture.

Keeping it all in the family, Gustav Stickley's own younger brothers, Leopold and J. George, brought him the greatest anguish by copying his designs. When the brothers didn't emulate their mentor, they were quite capable of developing quality products of their own. Their imprint, "The Work of L. and J. G. Stickley," indicated outstanding workmanship. Located in Fayetteville, they worked near their brother's Eastwood location with its Syracuse, New York, postal address.

Disturbed by the proliferation of idea snatchers, Stickley marked his pieces three times. One unique device he used was a joiner's compass of ancient vintage. Joiners predated cabinetmakers. In the days before glue and metal fasteners (such as nails or screws), these workers joined pieces of wood together to form furniture. They depended on wooden pegs (dowels), wedges, or special joints such as the mortise and tenon (which Stickley faked) to unite the parts. Between the prongs of his patented red joiner's compass, Stickley inserted a Dutch motto "Als ik Kan" which means "As I Can." Beneath this stamp he placed his first and last name. The Craftsman label comprised the other registered marking which was meant to protect the rights of both the designer and the purchaser. By the time his 1913 catalog was published, Stickley modestly declared that most of his furniture "was so carefully designed and well-proportioned…that even with my advanced experience I cannot improve upon it." Although his competitors helped drive him into bankruptcy in 1916, and he lived to see his plain furniture go out of style a few years later, his words were prophetic when he declared his furniture would be worth many times its original cost in fifty or one hundred years. Its scarcity and worthiness would make it so. That time is now. A child's rocker which retailed at $3.25 was priced at a low, low $165 at a recent antique show. An under fifty-dollar chest of drawers with Stickley's three marks might bring a couple of thousand dollars today. As the originator of an American style, he has been vindicated for his belief in austere furniture. How disturbing it must have been when his quality

Commode washstand, 30" wide, 18" deep, 28½" high, **$155-195.**

Craftsman furniture was lumped together with all other grades of functional oak furniture under the generic heading, "Mission." It's akin to forming a conglomerate of hand-blown, iridescent Tiffany and pressed, fading, gaudy goofus pieces.

The March 1912 issue of *Woman's Home Companion*, a magazine published by the Crowell Publishing Company, contained construction tips for three tables in Mission style with drawings by John D. Adams. Seasoned oak was the selected wood, while sharp tools and accurate measurements were listed as essentials. The home crafter could select a desk-table to fashion. An eight-sided pattern was versatile since it could be converted to a square or round top if desired, or be built in stool and taboret sizes. A folding table was suggested to save space in compact areas.

The Come-Pact Furniture Company, Toledo, advertised a Morris-look chair for $8.75, plus a library table for $11.75. Their quarter-sawed white oak had a good appearance in any of eight finishes, and customers could keep the articles on approval for one year. If they were dissatisfied, there was a money-back guarantee.

In that same magazine, George Edward Lewis revealed information in "How to Know Good Furniture." In the popularity race, oak was selected in seven out of ten orders. Thundering down the inside track, came mahogany followed by walnut, birch, maple, and oak look-alikes, ash and elm. The author recommended oak, mahogany, and walnut as first-rate woods that wouldn't readily shrink or warp. Besides, they had delightful patterns. "They are even-grained, can be carved, take a high polish, and wear well year after year." Lewis quickly dispensed with the Victorian Era's "fanciful scrollwork and machine carving." He felt the plain, straight lines of the Mission and other current styles deserved greater longevity. He felt the fumed look, accomplished (in his version) by placing furniture in a kiln filled with

Mission desk, drawer has pencil slot, inkwell, and lift-lid, 36" wide, 24" deep, 30" high, **$165-215.**

Child's mission rocker, **$65-85.**

Mission four-shelf bookcase, 17½″ wide, 11″ deep, 37″ high, **$75-110.**

Mission armchair, 24″ arm to arm, 35½″ high, **$75-95.**

Mission stool with leather top, 16½″ wide, 11½″ deep, 15″ high, **$55-75.**

burning straw, added unnecessary expense. To him, a hand-rubbed finish was preferable and more durable. Golden oak, antique mahogany, and satin walnut were favorites, but the darker stains lasted longer, the author stated.

The *Mother's Home Life* magazine for February 1925 contained an inviting advertisement. To those who would hurry to order the pictured, six-piece fumed oak set, a seven-piece genuine cut-glass water pitcher with tumblers would be sent

Mission library table, single drawer opens on both ends, 41½" wide, 25½" deep, 30½" high, **$165-195.**

Mission plant stand, top 12" square, 33" high, **$45-65.**

Mission plant stand, top 9½" square, 18" high, **$35-50.**

as a free bonus. The demand for Mission furniture was decreasing rapidly, and a new buying trend could be seen in the "I will trust you gladly" approach to installment buying. One dollar down and three dollars monthly with a full year to pay tempted housewives to go in debt for household furnishings. Another era was beginning. Credit merchandising was emerging.

Mission pedestal fern stand, top 9½″ square, 35½″ high, **$55-75.**

Mission swivel office chair, 24″ arm to arm, **$85-115.**

Mission swivel office chair, 24″ arm to arm, **$120-145.**

Mission armchair, 23″ arm to arm, 35″ high, **$85-115.**

Child's mission rocker, **$65-85.**

Mission armchair, upholstered seat, 26″ arm to arm, 37″ high, **$95-120.**

Lady's mission rocker, 33″ high, **$75-95.**
Small oak dovetailed toolbox, 13¼″ wide, 9¼″ deep, 10″ high, **$85-95.**

Mission rocker, upholstered seat, 26½″ arm to arm, 35½″ high, **$85-115.**

Ecclesiastical bench with cross in back and arm uprights, 46″ arm to arm, 41½″ high, **$350-400.**

Child's mission rocker, **$65-85.**

Liquor cabinet, top 18½″ square, 29½″ high, **$175-225.**

Same liquor cabinet with bottle compartment shown, 20″ extension above cabinet top. Compartment slides down and is hidden in rear.

Oval frame with fruit print, 30″ wide, 17½″ high, **$85-110.**

Frame with brass decorations on ends, fruit and game print, **$65-85.**

Mission bench, once used as a shoeshine stand in a barbershop, 62″ arm to arm, 38″ high, **$400-475.**

Child's Mission rolltop (curtain) desk, 26″ wide, 16″ deep, 36½″ high, **$175-225.**

Mission clock, 74½″ high, **$275-325.**

Mission doll bed, 13″ wide, 21½″ deep, 11″ high, **$65-85.**

7 The Bungalow and Its Built-ins

Are you tired of a giant house with lofty ceilings and extravagant features? Or, are you disgusted with life in a flat with shared halls and facilities? Why not move into an inexpensive toy house? These are questions that might have been asked in the early 1900s.

In his 1912 *Woman's Home Companion* article, "The Joys of the Bungalow," Francis E. Leupp extolled the virtues of these dwellings. It was an "appreciative" article. And with it were eight "Practical Bungalow Designs by Edwin Lundborg." Advantages? The small compact rooms did not permit the occupant to be messy. How small were the rooms? The limited space meant a person had to sit on the bed to open the drawers in his dresser. In this "toy house" there was no room for pack rats to retain collections, yet the owner enjoyed the privacy lacking in a flat (an apartment-building unit) where halls and functions frequently were shared.

While bungalows usually have only one story, they could have an upstairs. Often stout stone pillars, sometimes with boulders sunk in concrete, supported the roof of a rectangular front porch. (In the days before air conditioning, this was a social place.) Here children frolicked on hot days. "Of an evening" oldsters could gently sway in a swing or rocking chair and escape the excessive summer heat. When winter winds began to blow, the porch offered temporary shelter.

This type of home was available during a transition time when either oil or electric lamps might be present. Some areas had electric power while others did not, as this type of illumination was fairly new. For example, electricity was not installed in the White House until 1891, during Benjamin Harrison's term as President. Both he and his wife were suspicious of it. They summoned personnel to switch the lights on and off or frequently reverted to using the gas fixtures.

There were enticing interior features possible in bungalows, including thick exposed crossbeams on the ceilings. A 1912 *Woman's Home Companion* article suggested including built-ins. A fireplace could be flanked by seats or bookcases. Or, what could be a better place to curl up to read than a window seat in a bay?

Art glass panels made built-in china cabinets more colorful (see the photographs in the Color Section.) Chests of drawers or desks could be included in the floor plan. A buffet with storage space or a kitchen cabinet with shelves, drawers, extension top, breadboard, and flour bin might be as much a part of the petite house as its dark brown-stained woodwork and its rock and stucco outer surface, a common exterior for such homes.

As we mentioned earlier, Gustav Stickley, the man with so many talents, designed and built bungalows. Ceiling-scraping beds and dressers from the late Victorian years would not fit in these toy houses. Gustav Stickley's scaled-down functional furniture was comfortable in such rooms. He planned to have them complement one another.

8 A Little Bit about a Lot of Things

Pint-sized furniture for little ones has a special quality that attracts adult attention. Sometimes a question arises in an owner's mind. Is the miniature a salesman's sample (ss) or a child's possession? The draw table pictured here could be either; however, its knowledgeable owner labels it the former.

Draw table (either a salesman's sample or a child's table), 26" wide, 16" deep, 22" high, 8" leaves, **$165-215.**

Patented furniture was a vital part of the late 1800s industrial development. Beds folded into desks, chests, or wardrobes, while chairs rocked on all types of platforms or jolted on springs. High chairs could confuse baby by collapsing into a stroller or bed. The dainty cradle shown here is enhanced by beaded decorations applied to the surface. Look for patent dates on any mechanical furniture, as this means the piece was fashioned sometime after the last patent mentioned.

Other examples of tot-sized oakwares follow. Note how little pressed back chairs emulate those used by the parents.

Cradle on platform, 23″ wide, 42″ deep, 45½″ high. Shop price, **$695.**

Child's pressed back rocker, 28″ high, **$110-145.**

Child's pressed back rocker, 28″ high, **$110-145.**

Child's rocker, 28″ high, **$110-145.**

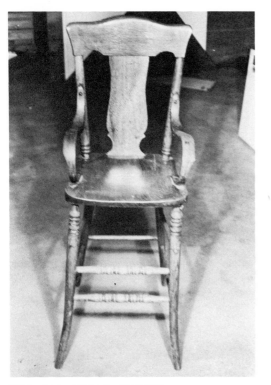

High chair, 41″ high, **$145-170.**

Pressed back high chair with tray, 41½″ high, **$175-225.**

Child's "Teddy" wagon, orange spoke wheels, slats form bed, 14″ wide, 36″ deep, **$165-210.**

Baby bed, 22″ wide, 39″ deep, 25″ high, **$185-225.**

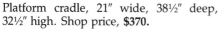

Platform cradle, 21″ wide, 38½″ deep, 32½″ high. Shop price, **$370.**

Mirrors with hat hooks were used by hostesses who lacked entry closets, which were not often included in house structures around the turn of the century. A guest could pat her hair in place upon arrival or put her bonnet on with care as she departed when the looking glass answered her query, "Mirror, mirror on the wall, am I fairest of them all?"

Hall mirror with three double hooks, 18″ square, **$135-150.**

Hall mirror with four double hooks, 23″ wide, 33″ high, **$175-215.**

School coat and hat rack, 24" wide, 6½" deep, label reads "Odell's Hat and Coat Rack, pat. Nov. 1, '87 mfg. by the Odell Iron Works, Indianapolis," **$90-115.**

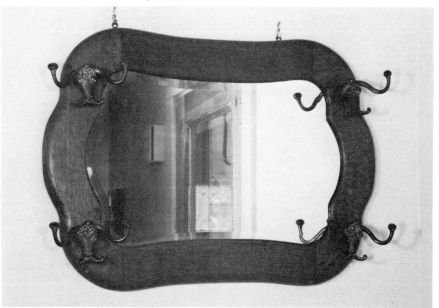

Hall mirror with four double hooks, 33" wide, 22" high, **$145-175.**

Hall mirror with four double hooks, 33½" wide, 21½" high, **$105-135.**

The family who owned the following piece called it "the bootery" because the aunt it came from placed it in her hall to hold outdoor footgear. The mirror *always hung over it.*

Closed bookcase, 30½" wide, 13" deep, 30" high, **$185-215.**

Framed mirror, 17½" wide, 31½" high, manufactured by Life Time Furniture, Grand Rapids Bookcase & Chair Co., Hastings, Michigan, **$110-135.**

Hall pier mirror, 25½" wide, 88" high, shelf depth 7½", **$995-1,095.**

A pier glass stands straight and tall, just like an English palace guard in his little niche, aloof from all passers-by. Originally such mirrors were placed between two windows, but later the term was stretched to include any long looking glass. Ash was frequently used in the late 1800 Victorian styles.

Cheval mirror used for shaving and makeup, 20″ wide, 9″ deep, 24½″ high, **$175-225.**

Burl-veneered oak mirror, 20″ wide, 29½″ high, **$45-65.**

Mirror with ornate gold-leaf liner, oak outer frame, 26½″ x 29½″ high, **$75-90.**

Double-framed mirror, 28½″ x 50½″, **$95-125.**

Wall mirror with applied decorations, 33" x 35½", **$55-75.**

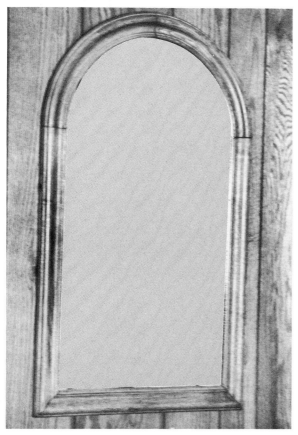

Molded and arched mirror, 21" x 36", **$75-95.**

To the separatist religious sect, the United Society of Believers, work was a form of worship. Perhaps that is why they produced furniture that was delightfully graceful, yet strong. "Shakers"—that's what they were called by others who watched them quiver as they danced before the Lord, men in one row, women in another, but never together. They were celibates. Skilled men made the frames for chairs while women were assigned seat-weaving duties. The sect, which lived apart from the world in their own communities, started selling chairs in the late 1700s and were among the first to construct chairs with rockers added. A size-numbering system was used after the mid-1800s, and a gold transfer trademark with the society's name identified their products. Ladder-backs (chairs with a series of slats across the backs in ladder formation) and woven seats were common, with frames constructed from native woods. Compare the delicate Shaker chair with the spindle-back chair shown here. Both are made of oak.

Shaker rocker, 22" arm to arm, 42" high, woven seat, **$350-400.**

Spindle-back rocker with splint seat, 39" high, **$145-165.**

Clocks can be squat or tall, round or rectangular. They can sit on shelves (mantel clocks do), hang on walls, or stand on the floor. Some even win beauty and

Label on back of the Ansonia clock showing its prize medal award at the Paris Exposition in 1878.

Ansonia wall clock, 13½″ wide, 5″ deep, 38″ high, **$375-425.**

performance awards, just as this Ansonia did back in 1878 at the Paris Exposition. Many had porcelain faces with fancy brass pendulums and glass doors with reverse painting. (The picture is painted on the back of the glass so that it will show correctly when the door is closed.) Some shelf varieties with fancy carvings have been dubbed "kitchen clocks." A regulator clock is supposed to be accurate.

Ansonia kitchen mantel clock, 14″ wide, 5″ deep, 22″ high, **$175-225.** Clock shelf, 25″ wide, 8″ deep, 10″ high, **$65-85.**

Seth Thomas eight-day mantel clock, 15″ wide, 4½″ deep, 23″ high, **$185-225.**

Eclipse eight-day wall clock, alarm, 14″ wide, 4″ deep, 28½″ high, **$225-250.**

Waterbury regulator clock with date hand, 16″ wide, 5″ deep, 34″ high, **$325-375.**

Ansonia wall clock, hinged at the top, not the side, 16″ diameter, 5″ deep, **$175-225.**

New Haven school regulator clock, 18½″ wide, 4½″ deep, 33½″ high, **$375-425.**

Wall clock marked "Std. Wa. Co., N. Y. pat., Feb. 25, '96," operated by electromagnet, 16" wide, 6" deep, 50" high, **$225-275.**

Seikosha wall clock, Japanese import, 9" wide, 4" deep, 18½" high, **$145-170.**

C. N. Welch regulator clock, 16" wide, 4½" deep, 38½" high, **$355-415.**

German box clock made after 1880, beveled glass shows pendulum, 16" wide, 5" deep, 38" high, **$325-375.**

Spices could be purchased at the store in hunks, as seeds, or in bulk form. Drawers of spice cabinets were marked with the names of the various types, and a mortar and pestle might be employed to pulverize the condiments into cookable, edible sizes. When these boxes are not relegated to the kitchen, they may hold sewing articles or form part of a wall grouping.

Spice box, **$95-115.**

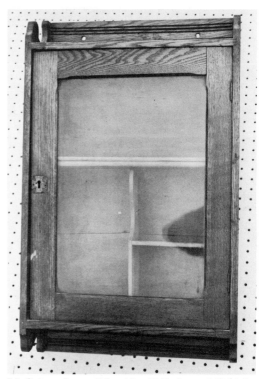

Medicine chest, 17″ wide, 5½″ deep, 28″ high, **$95-120.**

Medicine chest, 14½″ wide, 6″ deep, 18½″ high, **$55-85.**

Notice the fake bamboo appearance of this stand. The shelves are made of oak.

Criterion music box, 11½″ disks, 15″ wide, 14″ deep, 9″ high. Shop price, **$2,400.**

Whatnot stand, artificially grained shelf supports, ladder back to imitate bamboo, 16¼″ wide, 11½″ deep, 36½″ high, **$75-95.**

Edison phonograph, latest patent Nov. 17, 1903, 13″ wide, 9″ deep, 11½″ high. Shop price, **$495.**

Who doesn't enjoy the tinkling tones of a music box? The Swiss invented a type with revolving cylinders in the early 1800s. But only a certain number of tunes would play on that particular box, perhaps four, eight, ten, or twelve. That was it, then. Patents in the latter part of the century were taken out on disk types. On these, metallic sheets with their perforations could be changed at will so that one box could play any tune sheet available in a specific size. What an improvement this was. But it was "instruments only" until Thomas A. Edison invented the first successful "talking machine" in 1877. Now the human voice could be heard on records. It was necessary to wind these machines with an attached hand crank. Sounds carried forth through a large, trumpet-shaped horn.

Graphophone made by Columbia Phonograph Co., latest patent March 30, 1897, 12″ wide, 7½″ deep, 7″ high. Shop price, **$650.**

Victrola made by Victor Talking Machine Co., sold by Pa Stack Piano Co., Chicago, Ill., **$265-325.**

Epworth organ made by Williams Organ Co., Chicago, Ill., 55″ wide, 30″ deep, 46½″ high, **$795-895.**

This organ with its delicate fretwork and incised carving is an Epworth, made by the Williams Organ Company in Chicago. Besides having musical ability, a player needed strength to pump the pedals with his feet, provide proper knee action, move his fingers over the keys, and pull out the necessary stops. That's coordination plus. Sing-alongs were always popular in the parlor. Some organs were equipped with swing-out stands to hold candles or lamps that permitted the organist to see with ease.

Piano bench converted to a coffee table, 39" wide, 19" deep, 21" high, **$65-95.**

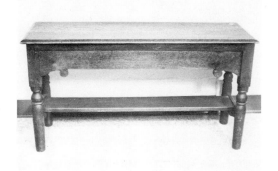

Piano bench, lift top, 40½" wide, 13½" deep, 21" high, **$75-95.**

Armchair rocker, 23" arm to arm, 35" high, **$115-145.**

Armchair rocker with veneered seat, 26" arm to arm, 40" high, damaged veneer, **$65-85.**

Available in golden or fumed oak finish (or at times, artificially grained) these oak chairs display some transitional features. Curves were added to the straight stocky Mission lines. They are about late 1920s in vintage. Women who sat in them probably cut their long, twisted-back hair into a short, "bobbed" look. Dresses no longer brushed the floor, but were knee-length. Autos roared on rutted roads. Life was faster paced, and swift dance steps were in vogue, as was buying on credit with time payments. Electricity was beginning to light up the cities.

Armchair rocker, 24½″ arm to arm, 40″ high, **$125-165.**

Armchair rocker, upholstered back and seat, 26″ arm to arm, 41″ high, **$85-115.**

Armchair rocker, upholstered back and seat, 25½″ arm to arm, 38″ high, **$175-225.**

Child's rocker, 21″ arm to arm, 29″ high, **$90-120.**

Office chair, **$115-130.**

Office chair, handhold in back rail, **$85-110.**

Office chair, **$65-95.**

A sign of today's times is the invasion of English furniture. The scrub top table pictured here is circa 1920 with leaves that fold double on the top. The leaves can be pulled out and dropped when a larger surface is needed.

Scrub-top table, 30" wide, 36" deep, 30½" high (in closed position), **$265-315.**

Below: scrub-top table with one end pulled out to extend 15". Total extension, 30".

This dresser has bail handles with pot metal backplates that cannot be joined together once they are broken or rent asunder.

English dressing stand, 42" wide, 19½" deep, 61½" high, **$375-450.**

Twin bed, circa late 1930s, overall width 42", overall length 83". An antique of the future.

Antique of the future? Perhaps that's the title that should be applied to this 1930s draw table and oak twin bed.

Draw table, circa late 1930s, 44" wide, 30" deep, 30" high, 10" extension on each end, **$165-195.**

Oval mirror frame for decorative family tree, 20″ wide,
40″ high, **$35-55.**

Here, an oval frame now holds a family tree instead of a mirror.

Frame, gold-leaf insert, oak outer frame, 27½" wide, 31½" high, **$65-85.**

Frame with decorative gold trim outlining, 17" wide, 20" high, **$65-85.**

Leaders of the Arts and Crafts Movement felt that a home should have beauty and peace. This, in turn, would contribute to the moral growth of the individuals who resided there. This motto seems to embody that spirit and provides a fitting closing to a book that includes a chapter on furniture with a mission.

Godly House Blessings

Where there is faith, there is love
Where there is love, there is peace
And where there is peace, there is blessing
Where there is blessing, there is God
And where God is—there is no need.

Frame with gold-leaf liner surrounding German religious motto, 17½" wide, 20½" high, **$65-95.**

Glossary

applied carving   an ornament crafted separately and added to a piece of furniture.

apron   the connecting piece on chairs, cabinets, and tables (see skirt).

artificial grain   paint or stain applied to imitate the grain of a specific wood.

bail handle   a metal half-loop drawer pull attached to a backplate.

buffet (sideboard)   a piece of furniture for storing silverware, dishes, linens, or other tableware in a dining area.

bulbous   bulb-shaped. Frequently used to describe a plump, highly carved leg.

cabriole leg   a leg with a double curve flowing out at the knee, in at the ankle, then slightly outward again.

chamfer   a corner or edge cut off to form a slanting surface.

cheval mirror   a swinging looking glass supported by an upright frame. A cheval dresser has a large mirror of this type, usually set to one side of the hat cabinet.

chiffonier   a tall, narrow chest of drawers.

chip carving   simple carved decoration made with a chisel or gouge.

circa   an approximate date. Most of the furniture in this book is circa 1900.

claw feet   furniture feet which resemble an animal's paws.

commode   enclosed cupboard-type washstand.

cornice   top, horizontal molding on furniture.

crest   a carved piece on the top rail of a sofa or chair.

cylinder   a curved sliding top on a desk or secretary. Also, a desk or secretary which has such a rounded front.

drop lid or front   a hinged lid on a desk which drops down to form a writing surface.

eclectic   adapting and combining designs and styles of various periods.

extension table   a table top that pulls apart so leaves may be added to enlarge it.

gargoyle   originally a grotesquely carved ornamental creature projecting from a building. Such a carving on furniture.

hardware   metal used on a piece. This includes nails, screws, hinges, and the like. Pulls and handles are called hardware even when they are made of glass, ceramic, or other material.

Hoosier   generic name for a kitchen cabinet with a pullout work surface, meal or flour bins, drawers, sifters, cupboard space, etc. This one-unit cabinet was made in the late 1800s and early 1900s in the Hoosier state, Indiana, and elsewhere. Different companies used other names.

incised   a design cut into the surface.

marriage   pieces of furniture combined as one when they were not originally a single unit. Example: a bookcase top added to a drop-front desk to form a secretary.

mortise and tenon   the mortise is a slot or hole in a piece of wood. A tenon is a protruding tongue or prong in another piece of wood which fits snugly into the mortise to form a tight joint. They may be pegged where they join.

pier glass or mirror   a tall narrow mirror often hung between two long windows.

plank seat   a solid, wooden seat. In older chairs, the seat was frequently one piece of wood.

pressed back   a design pressed into the back of a chair with a metal die to imitate carving.

rolltop   a flexible hood that slides down as a rounded lid on a desk.

rung   a crosspiece that connects cabinet, chair, or table legs at the bottom (also called stretcher or runner).

scalloped   a series of curves in an ornamental edge patterned after the shape of a shell.

sideboard   see buffet.

Shakers   a religious community which constructed and sold plain, attractive, strong furniture to the public.

skirt   the connecting piece on chairs, cabinets, and tables. In chairs, it is beneath the seat; on tables, underneath the top; on cupboards and chests, it is at the bottom between the feet. It can hide construction details or add support (also called apron).

slant front   the hinged drop lid on a desk or secretary that provides a writing surface when opened.

slat   horizontal crossbar in chair backs.

splat   the center upright in a chair back.

splay   slant out, especially chair legs which slant from the seat to the floor.

stile   the vertical piece in a frame or panel in furniture.

stretcher   see rung.

taboret (tabourette)   a small plant stand.

turning   shaping wood with chisels on a lathe to form table and chair legs or other items.

veneer   a thin layer of decorative wood glued over the surface of a cheaper wood.

wardrobe   a piece of furniture in which garments were hung before closets were common.

Bibliography

Aronson, Joseph. *Encyclopedia of Furniture*. New York, N.Y.: Crown Publishers, Inc., 1965.

Cole, Ann Kilborn. *How to Collect the New Antiques*. New York, N.Y.: David McKay Company, Inc., 1966.

Durant, Mary. *The American Heritage Guide to Antiques*. American Heritage Publishing Co., Inc., 1970.

1897 Sears, Roebuck Catalogue. Fred L. Israel, editor. New York, N.Y.: Chelsea House Publishers, 1976.

Grotz, George. *The New Antiques*. Garden City, N.Y.: Doubleday & Company, Inc., 1964.

Mackay, James. *Turn-of-the-Century Antiques*. New York, N.Y.: E.P. Dutton & Co., Inc., 1974.

1927 Sears, Roebuck Catalogue. Alan Mirken, editor. New York, N.Y.: Bounty Books division of Crown Publishers, Inc., 1970.

Sears, Roebuck & Co. 1908 Catalogue No. 117. Joseph J. Schroeder, Jr., editor. Chicago, Illinois: The Gun Digest Company, 1969.

Stickley Craftsman Furniture Catalogs, Craftsman Furniture Made by Gustav Stickley and *The Work of L. & J. G. Stickley*. Introduction by David M. Cathers. New York, N.Y.: Dover Publications, Inc., 1979.

Index

About the Authors

Bob and Harriett Swedberg especially enjoy collecting antiques because of the fine friendships they have made with others who share this interest. This hobby links the generations, binds various nationalities together, and spans economic barriers. The Swedbergs like to share their knowledge through teaching classes, conducting seminars, lecturing, and exhibiting items at antiques shows. These Moline, Illinois, residents are members of "Speakers' Corner" (309-794-0505) and are available for programs. They have written columns and have been featured guests on many radio and television programs.